Happy Halloween

NAME : ....

AGE : ....

DATE : ....

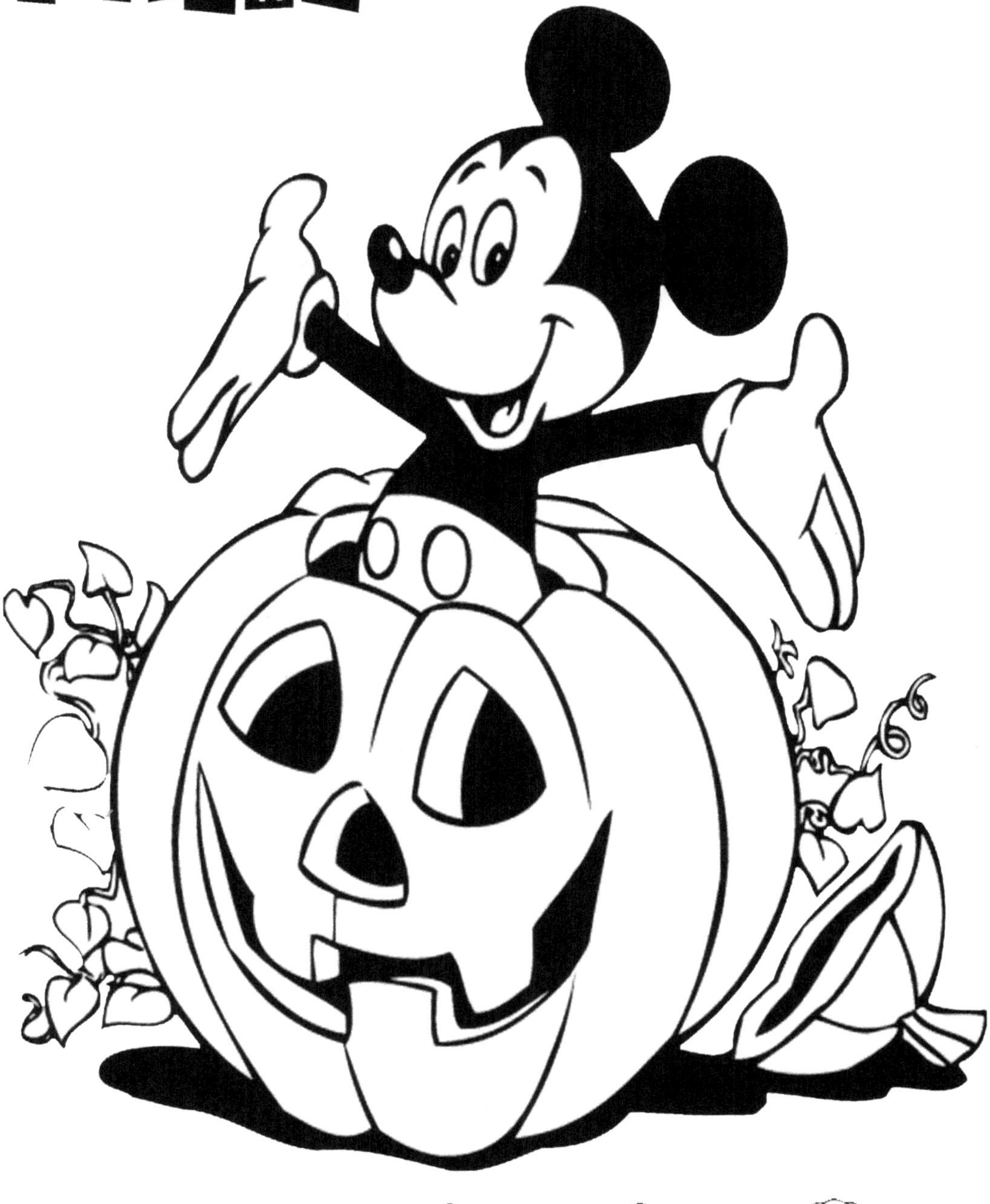

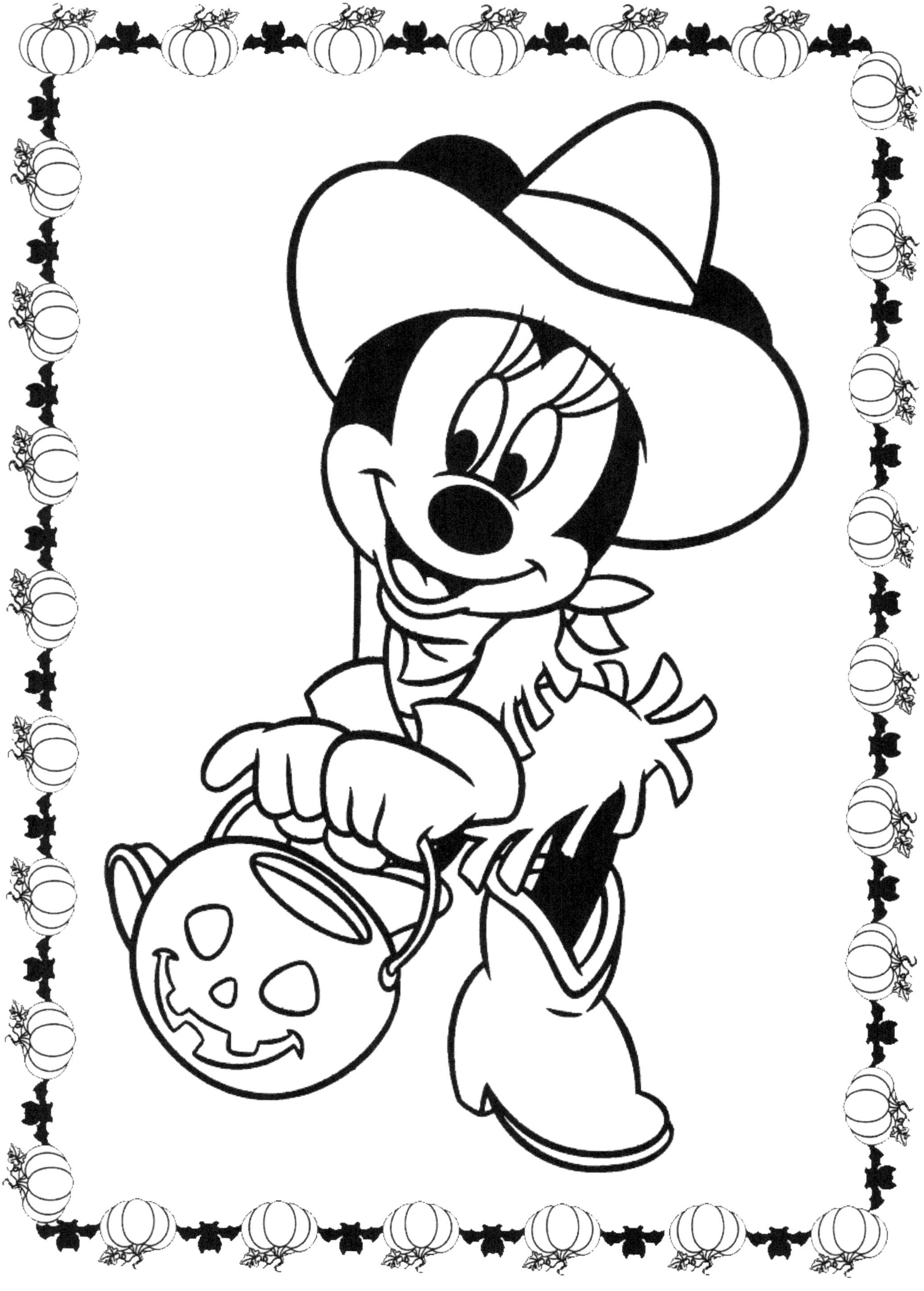

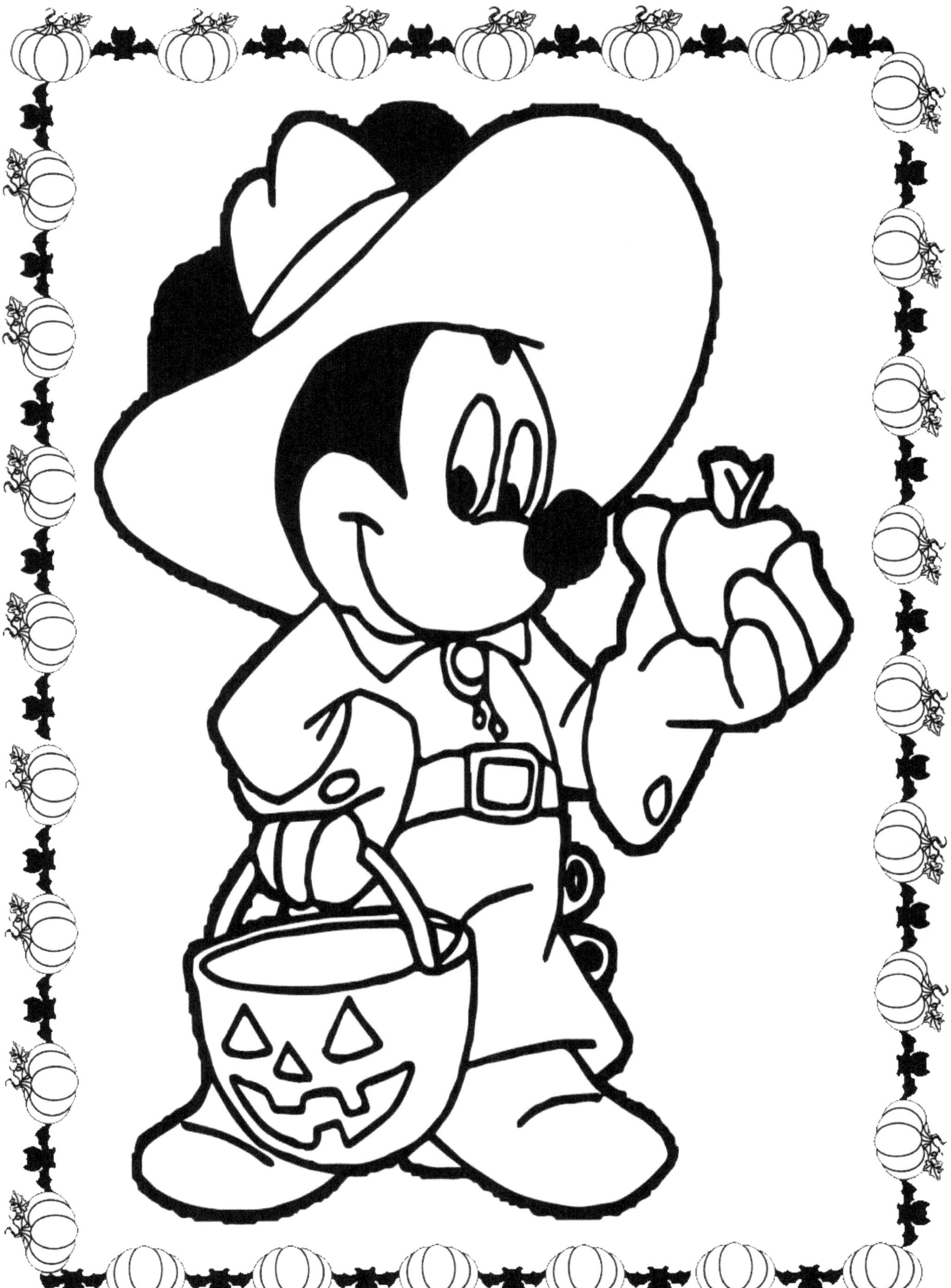

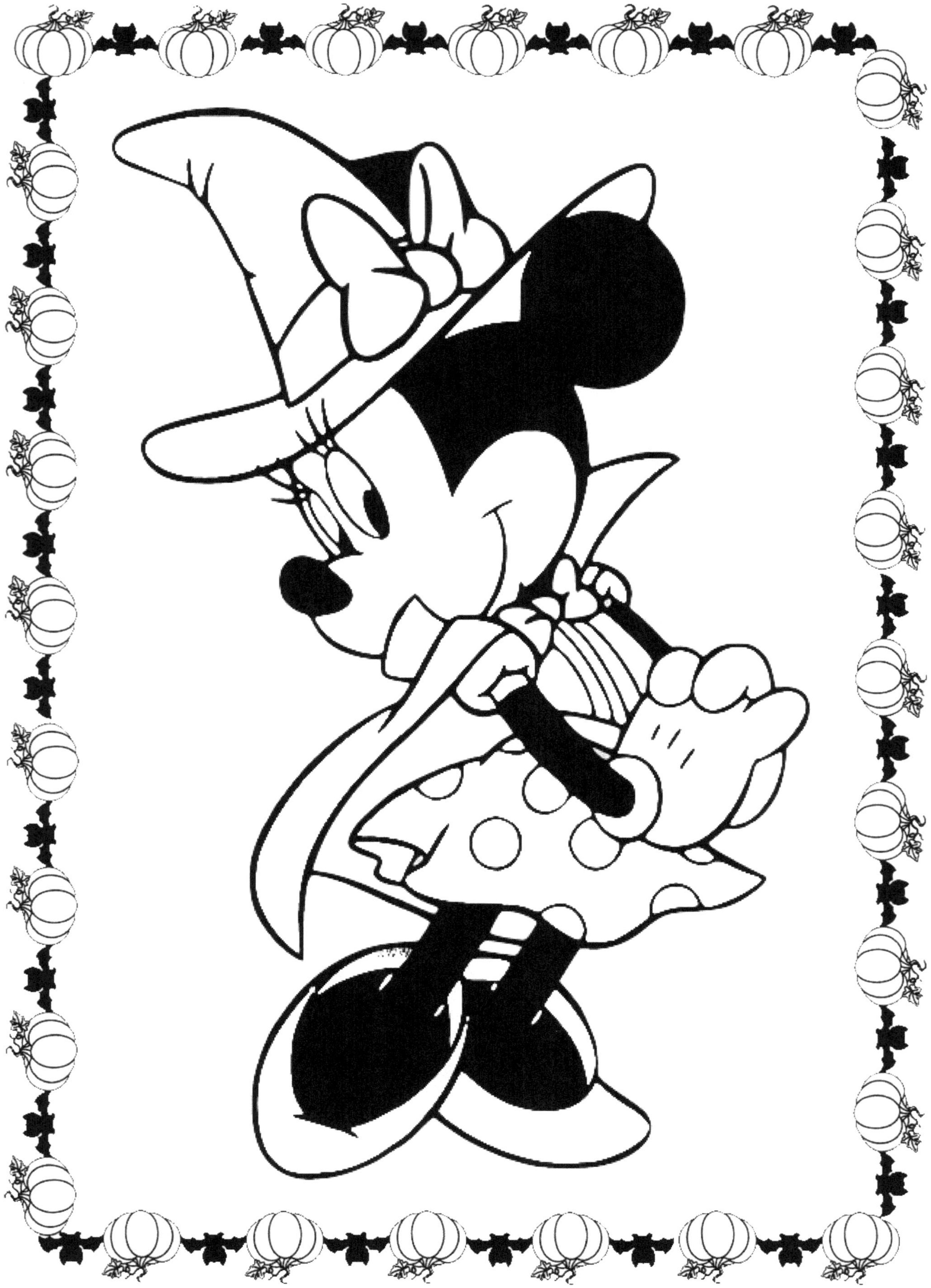

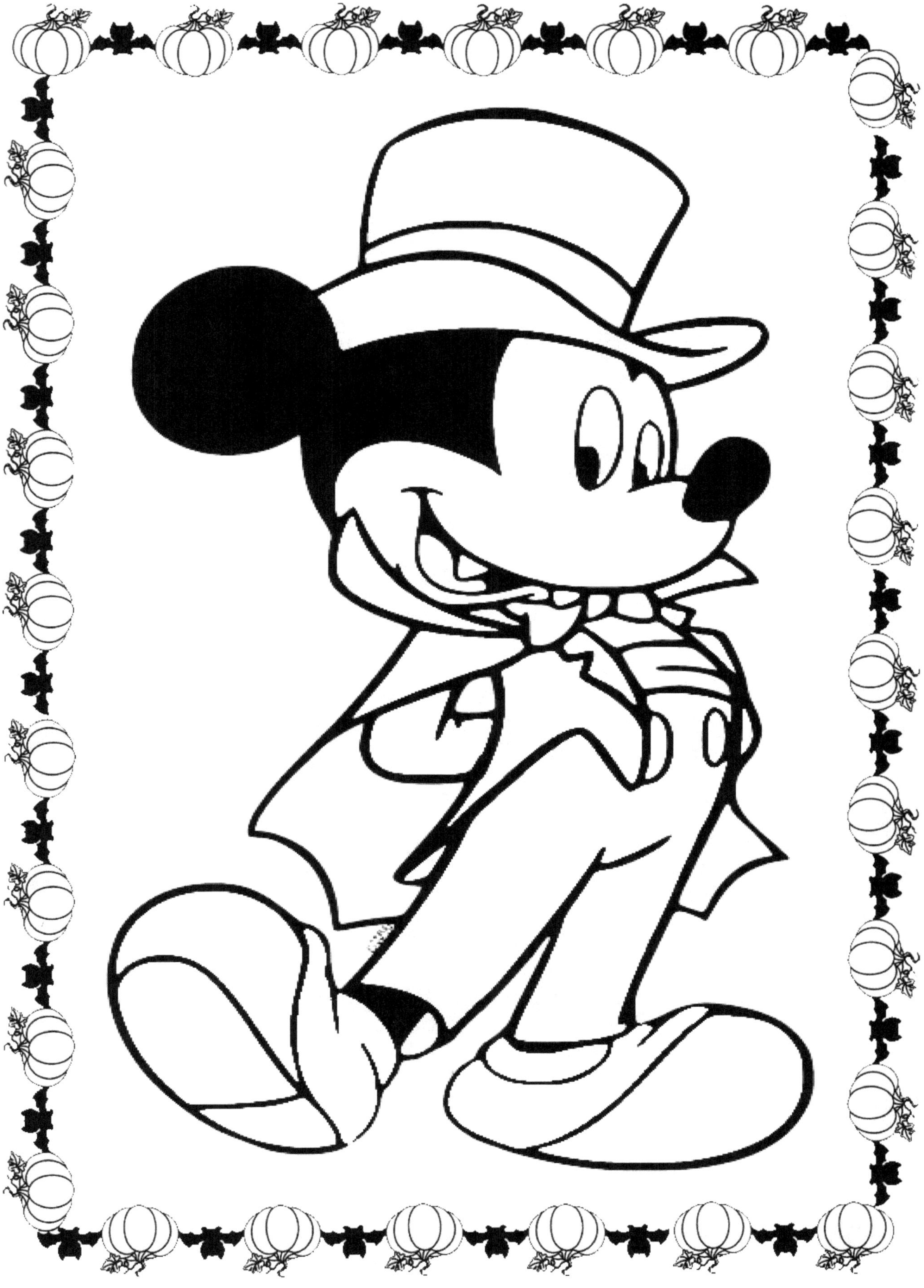

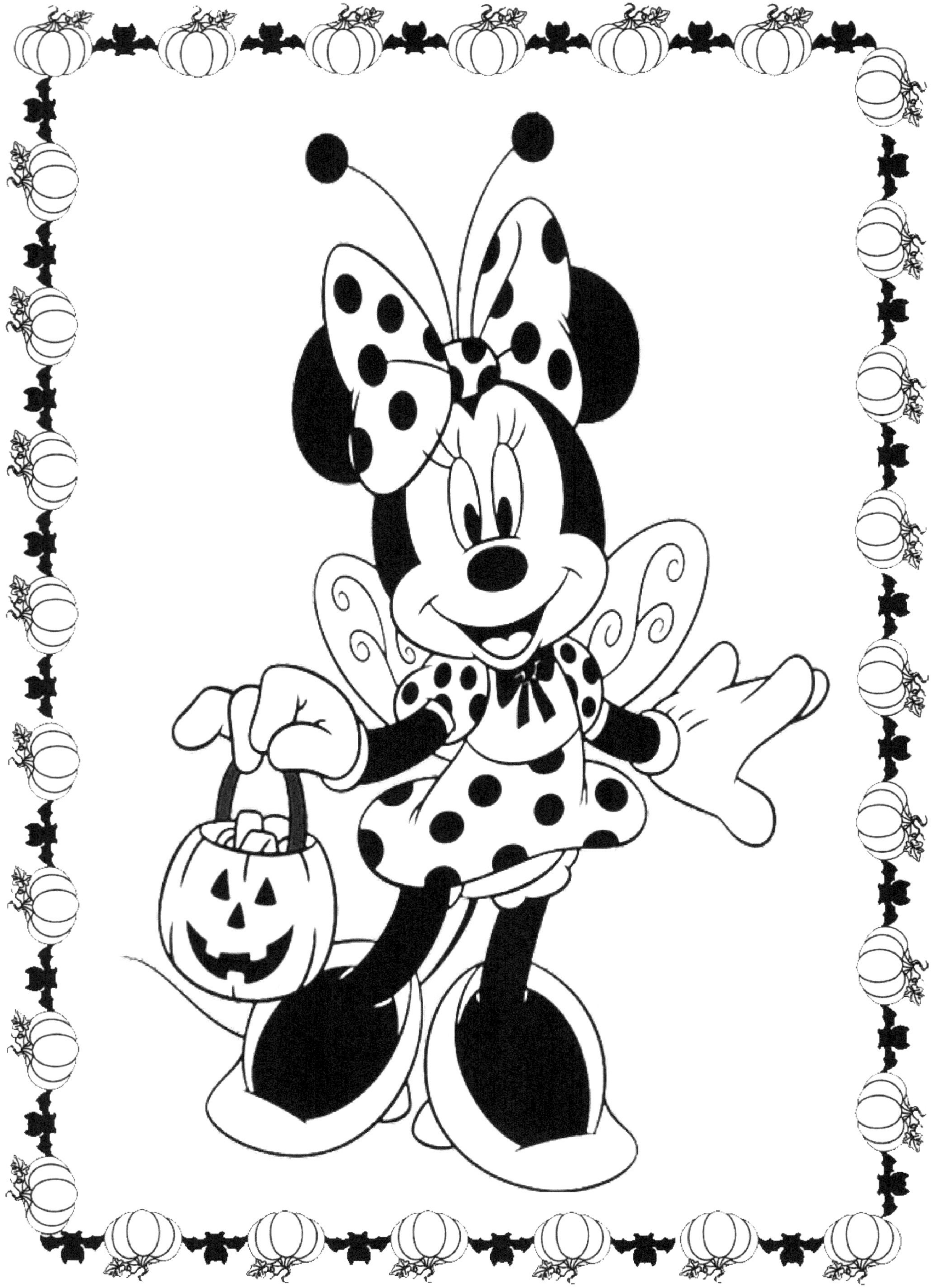

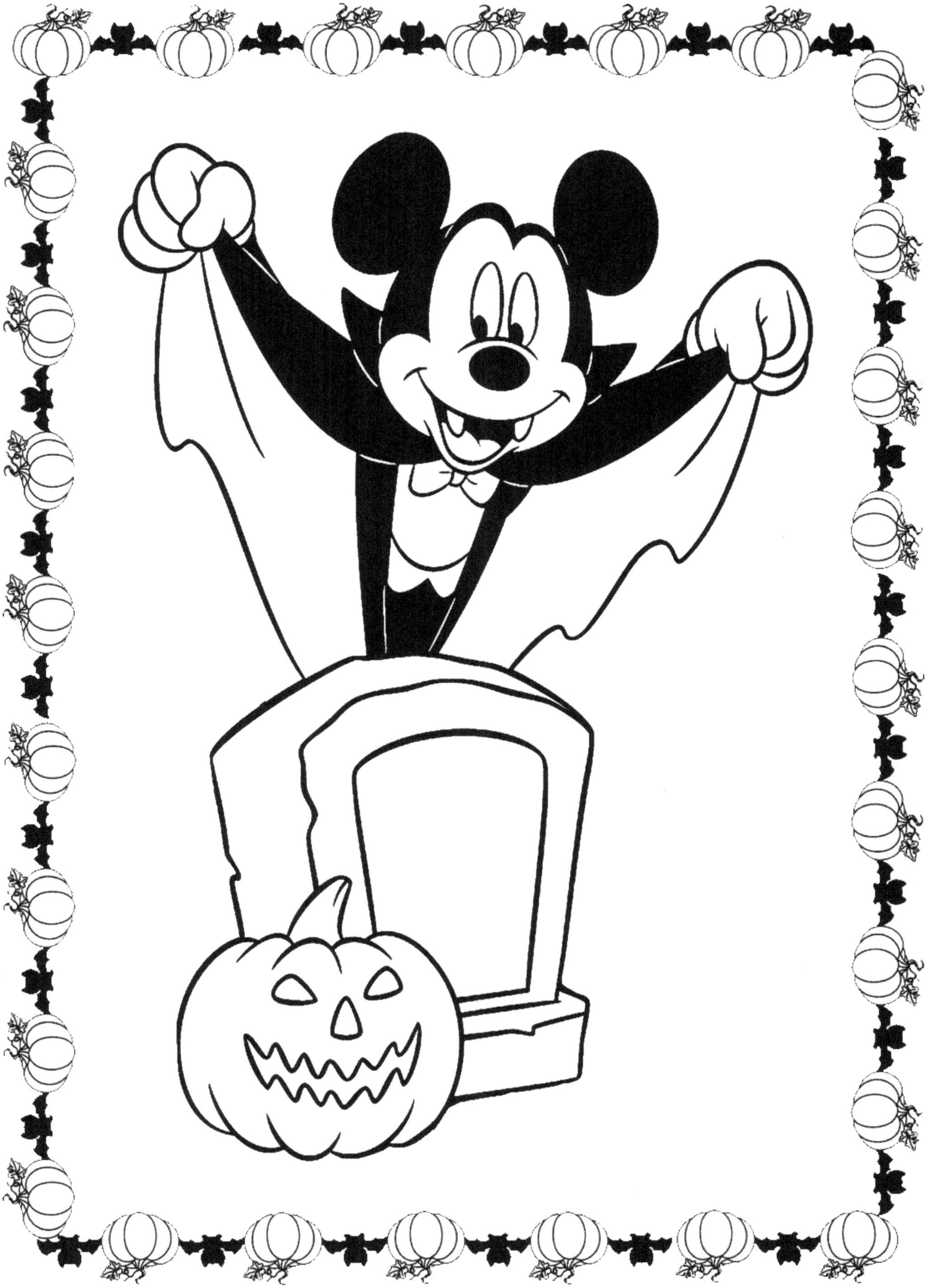

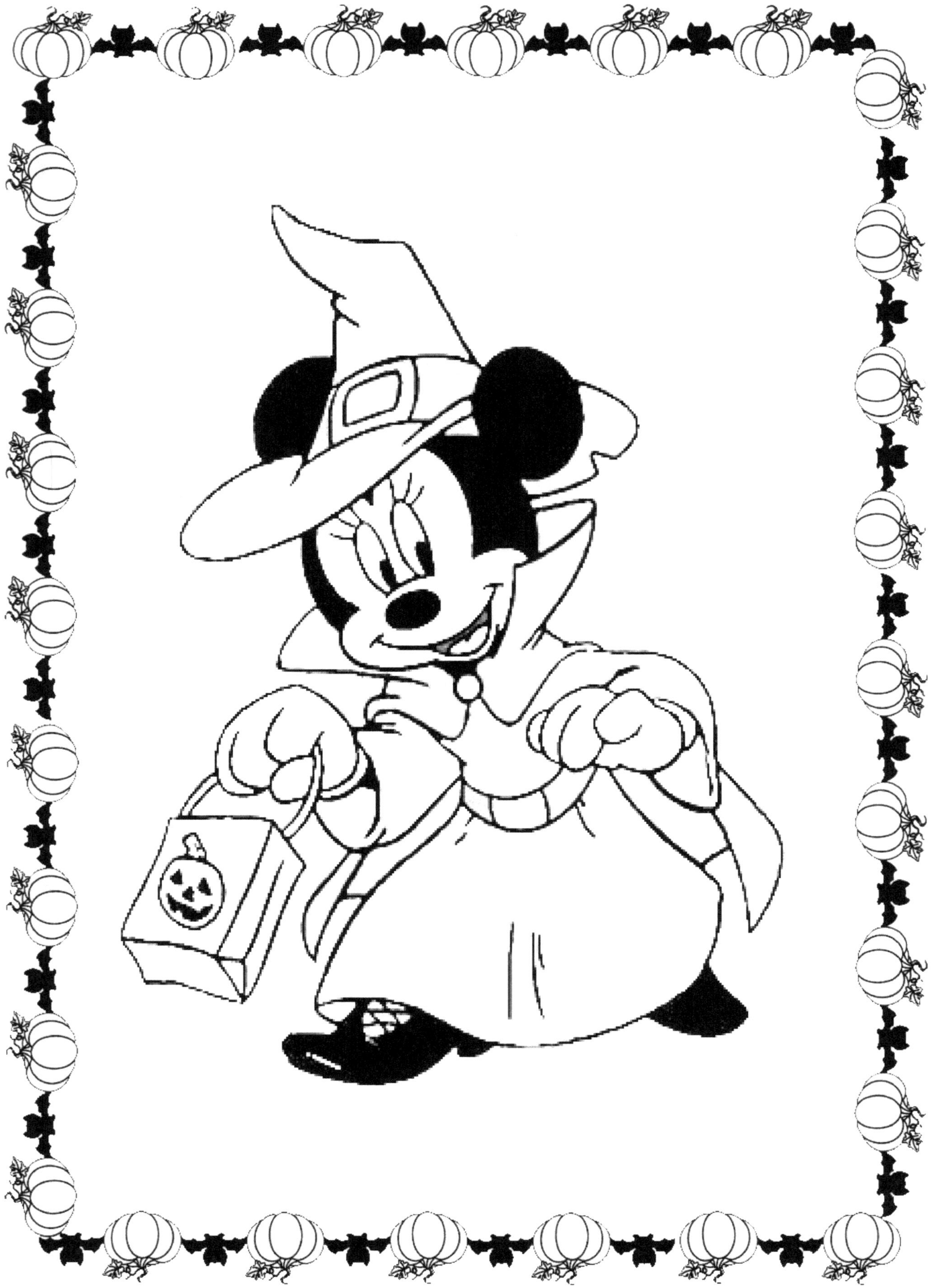

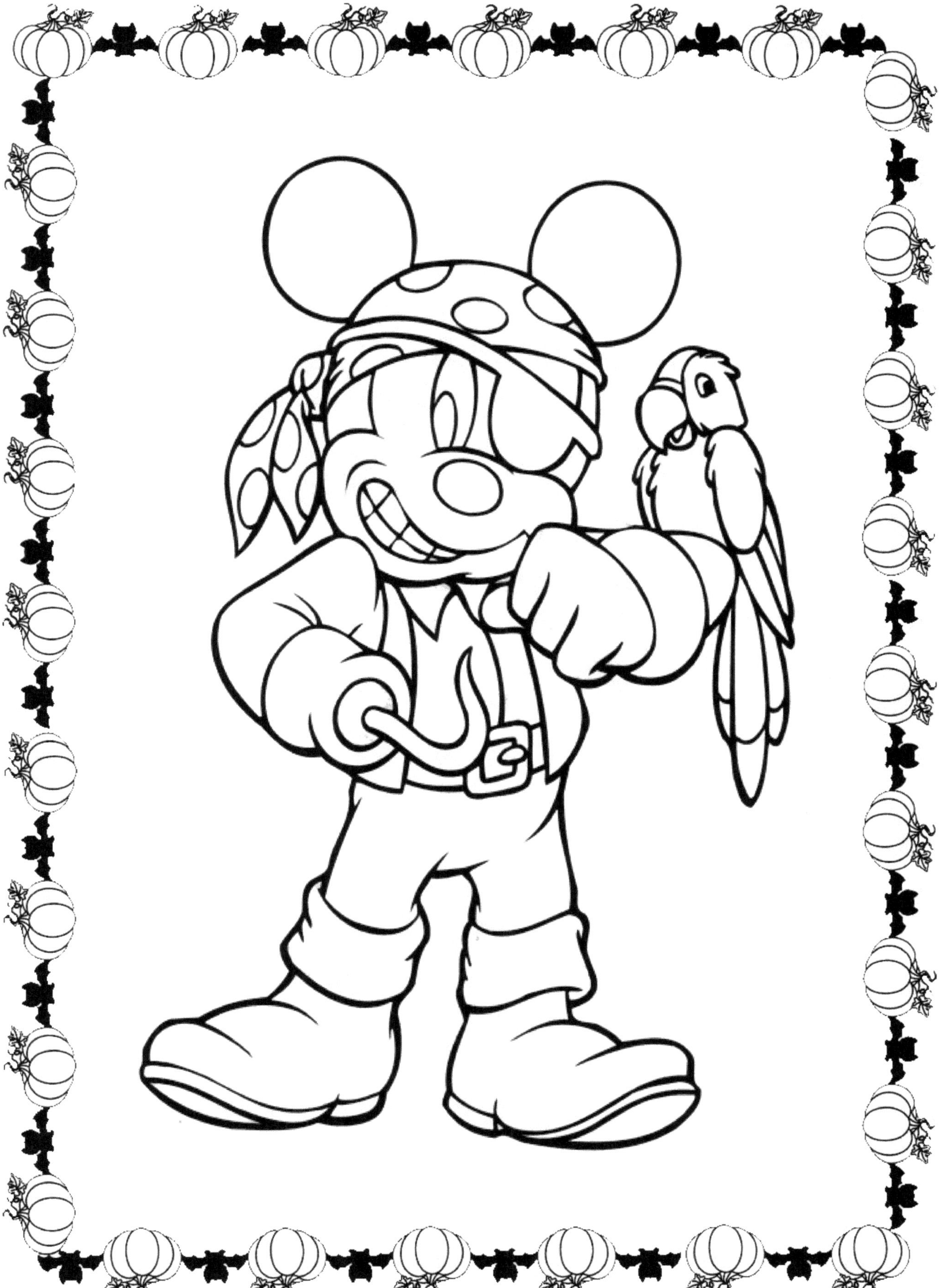

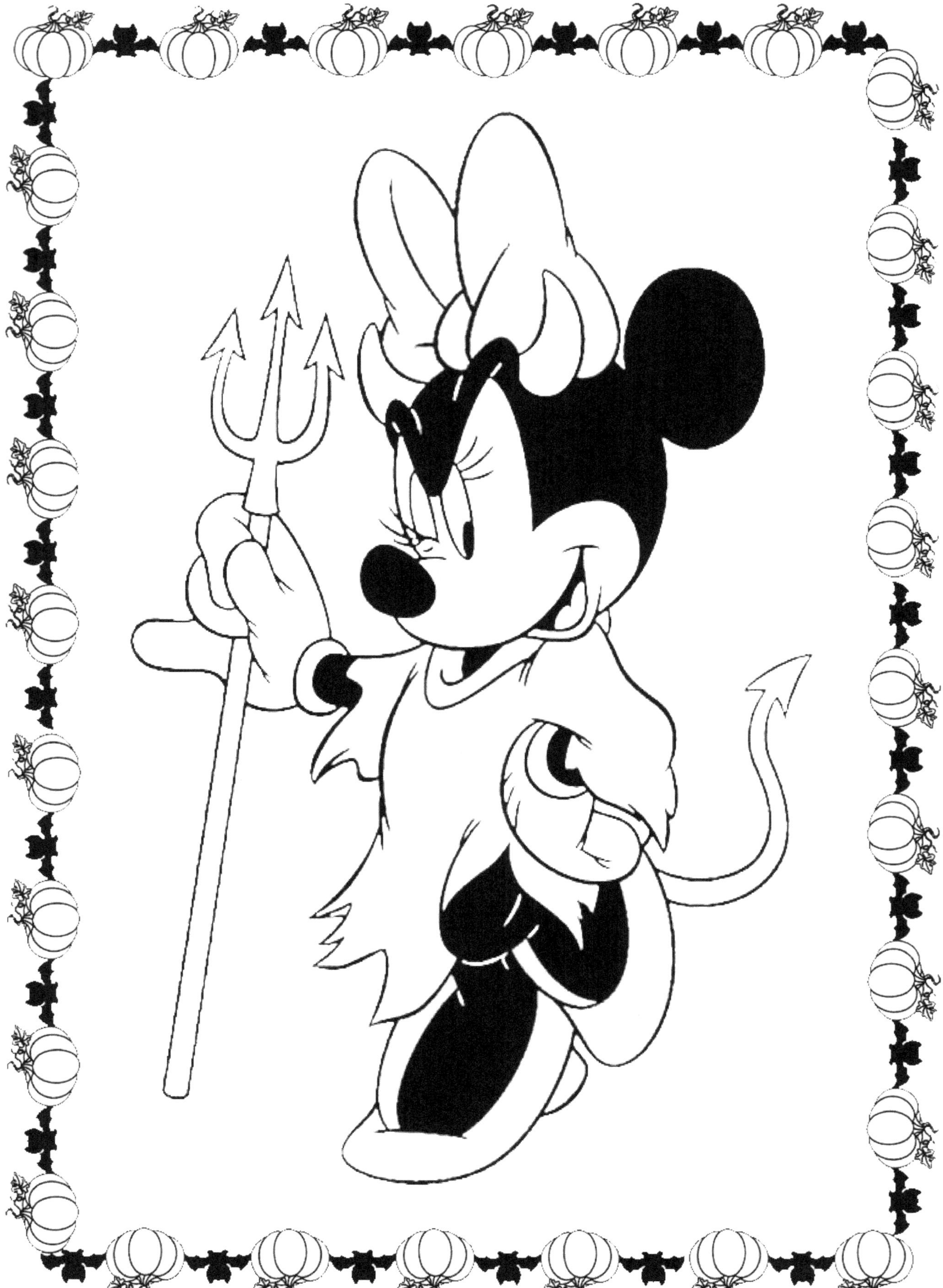

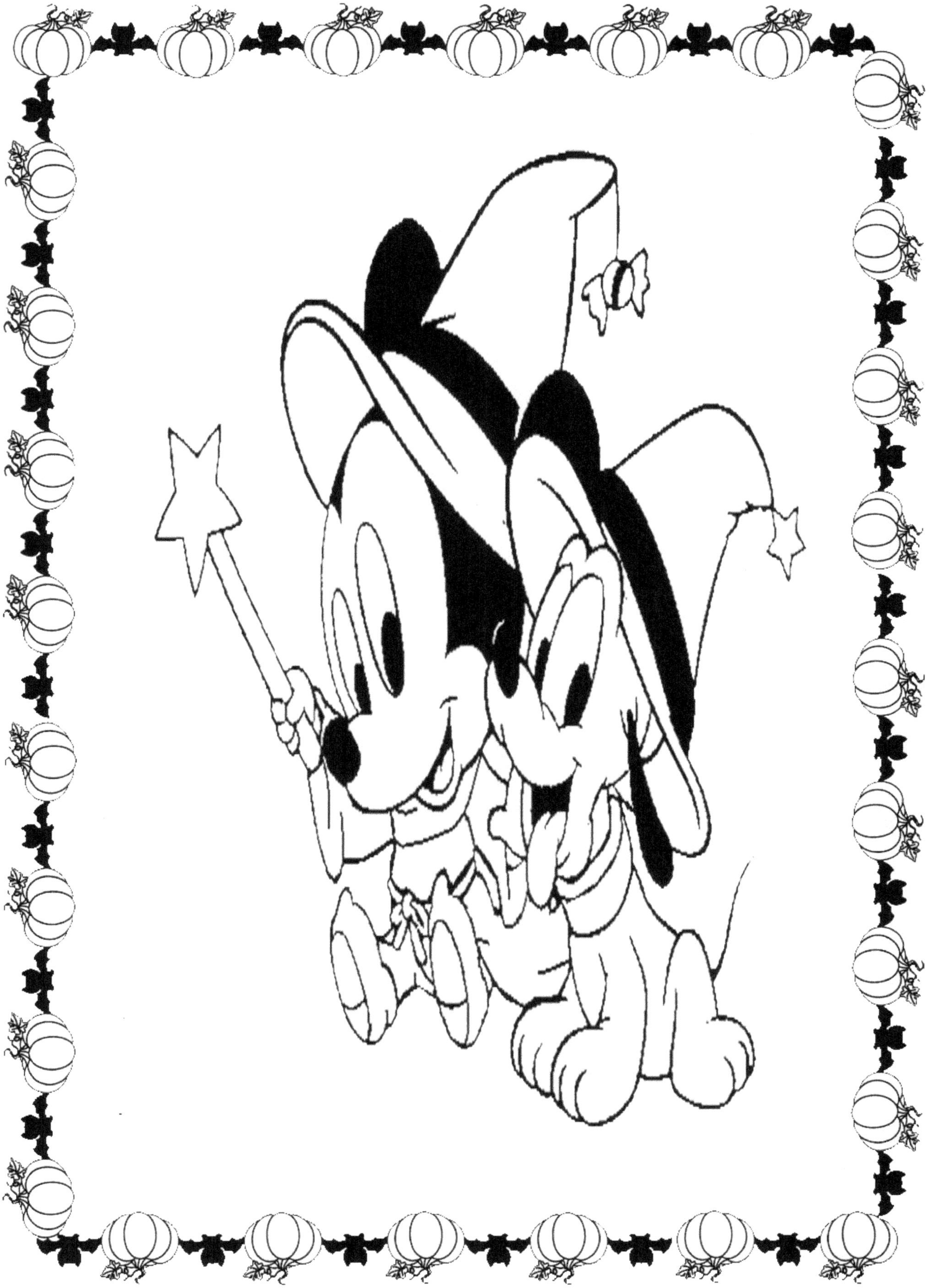

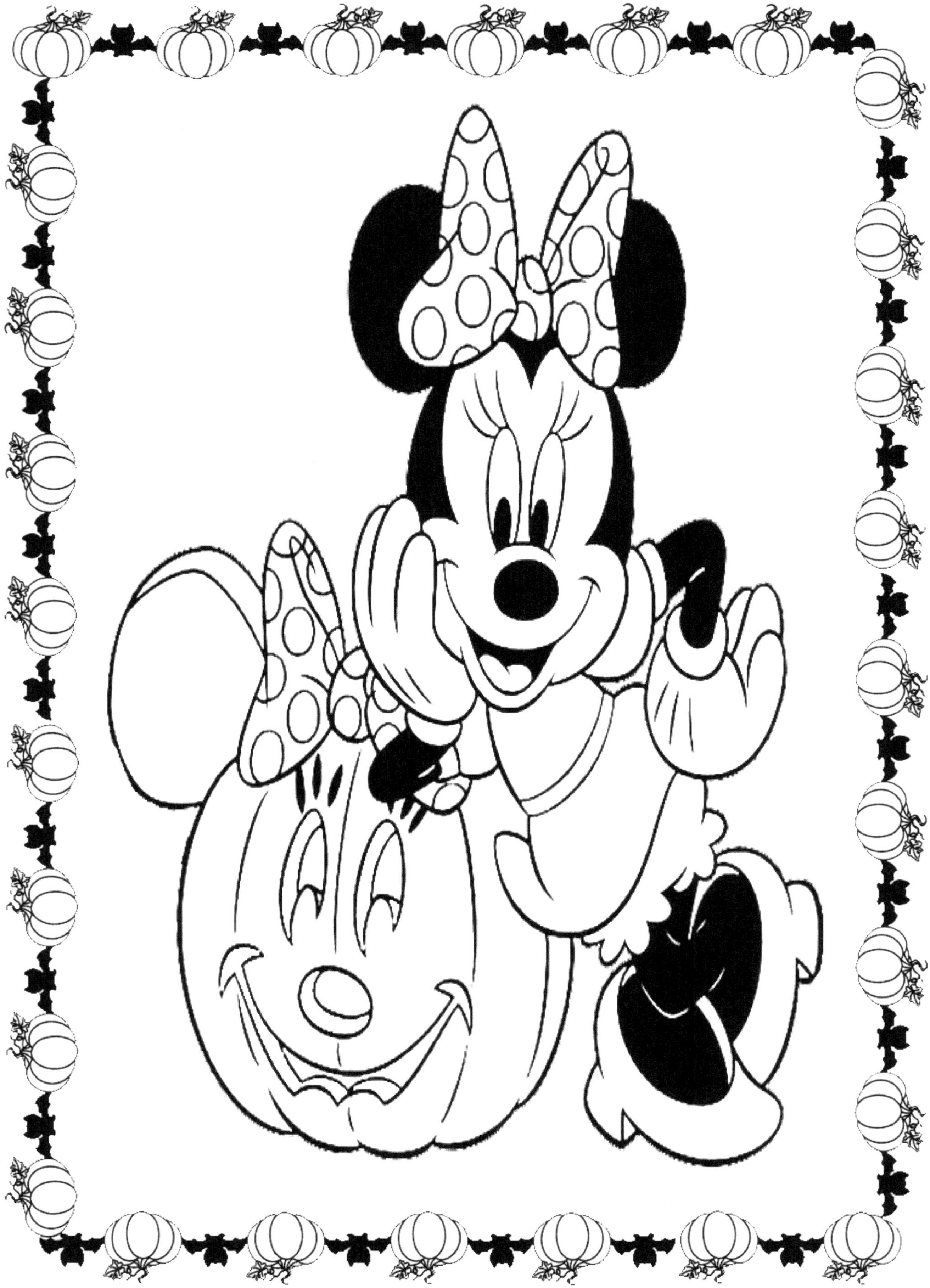

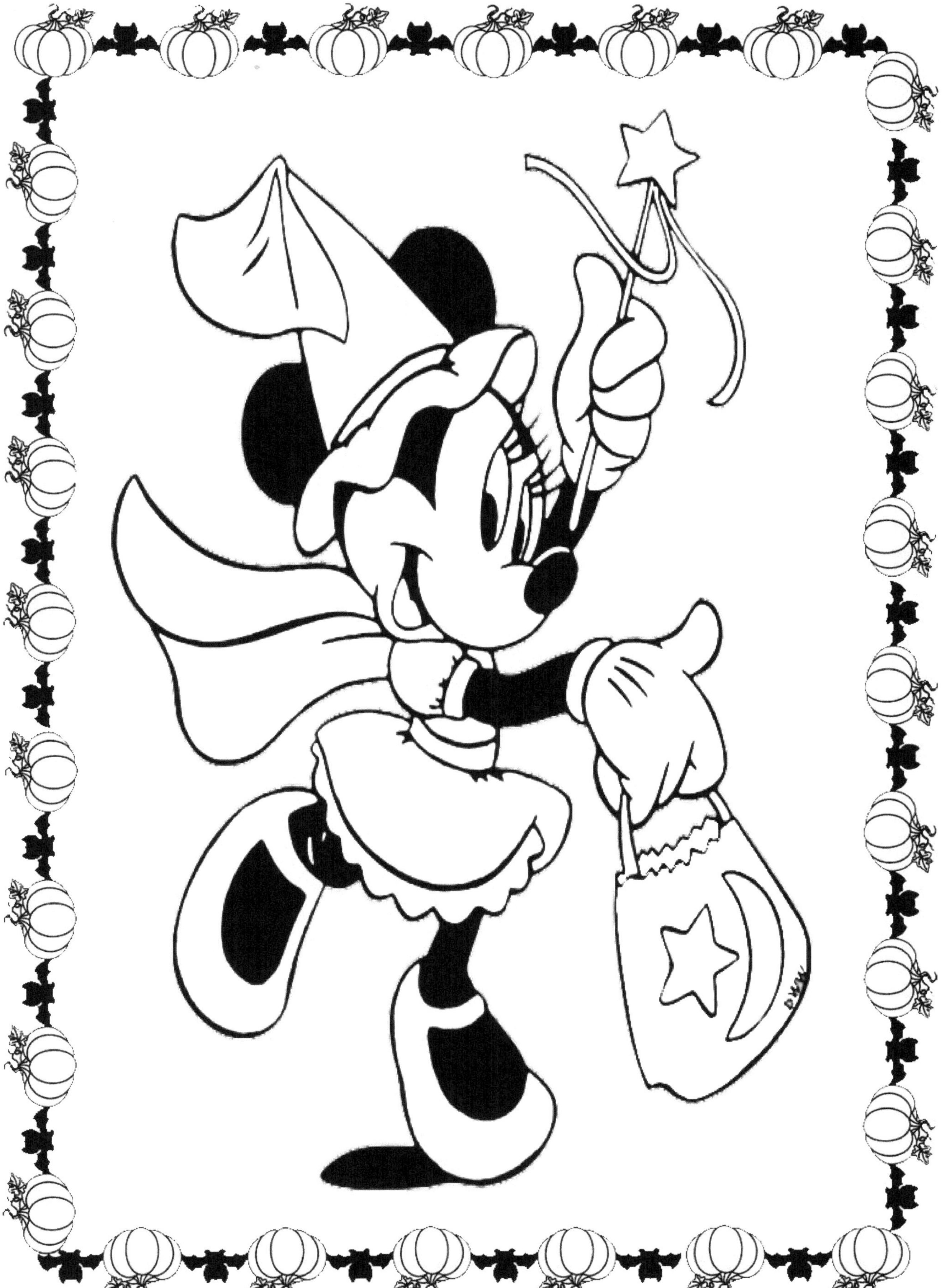

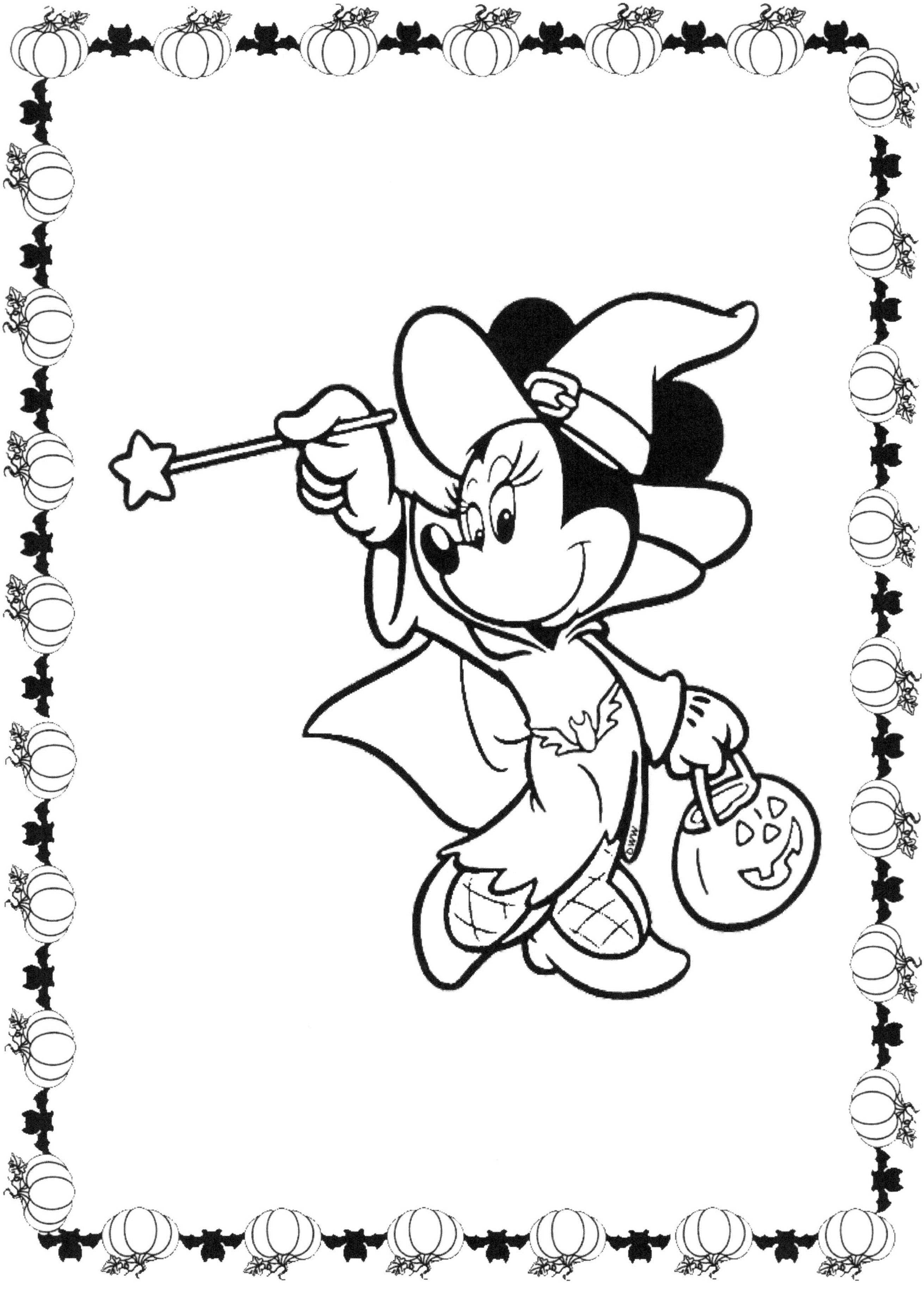

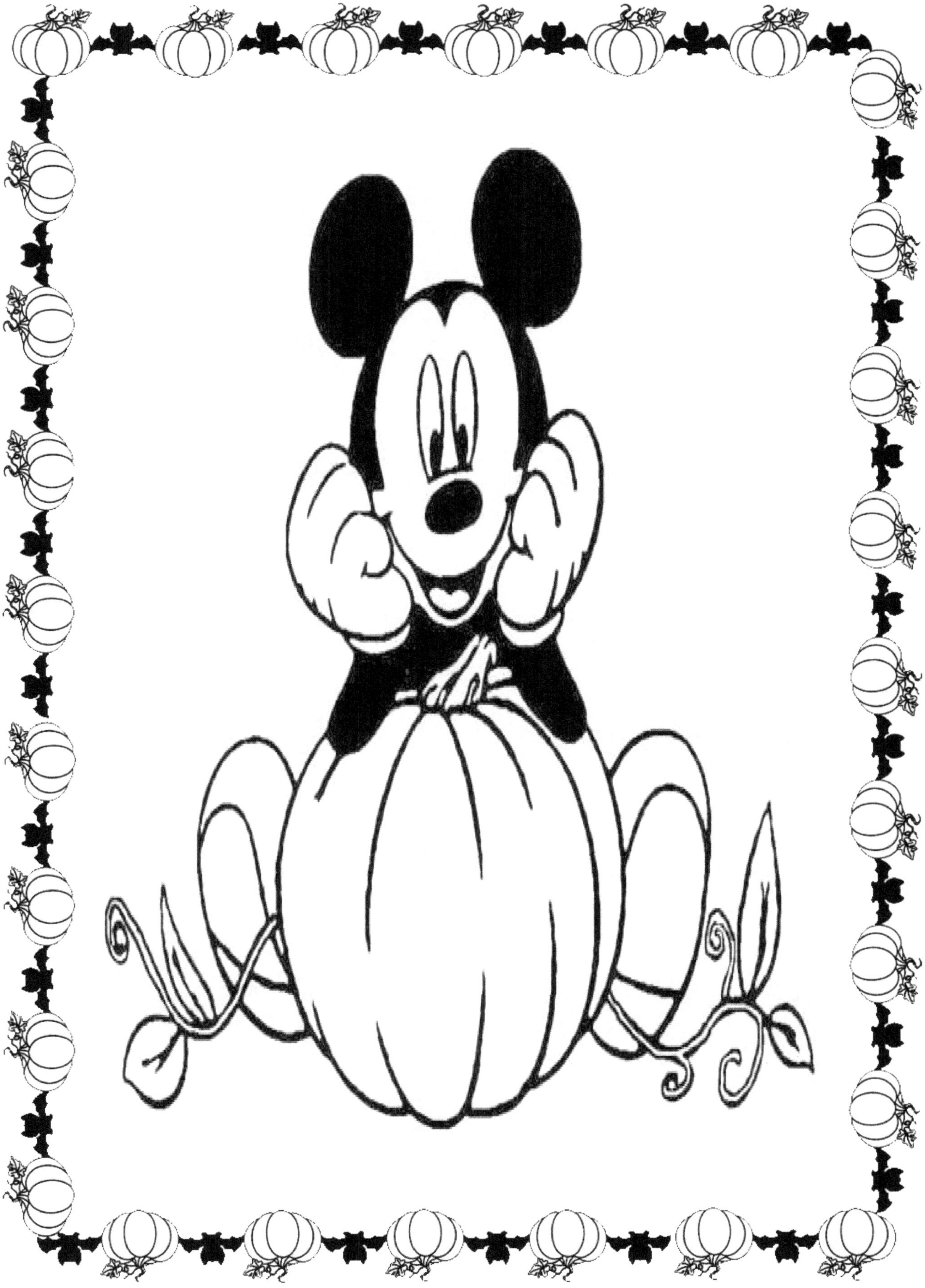

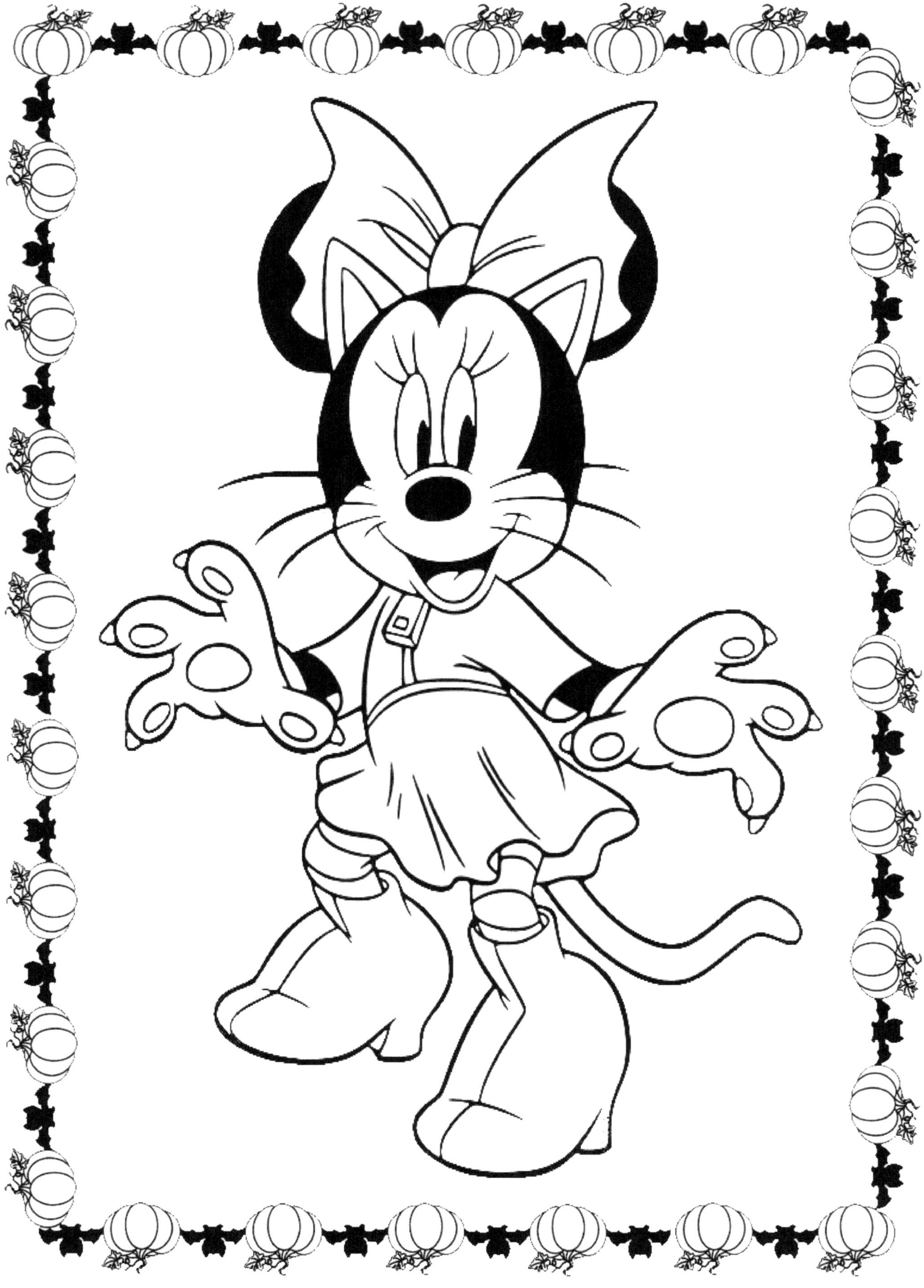

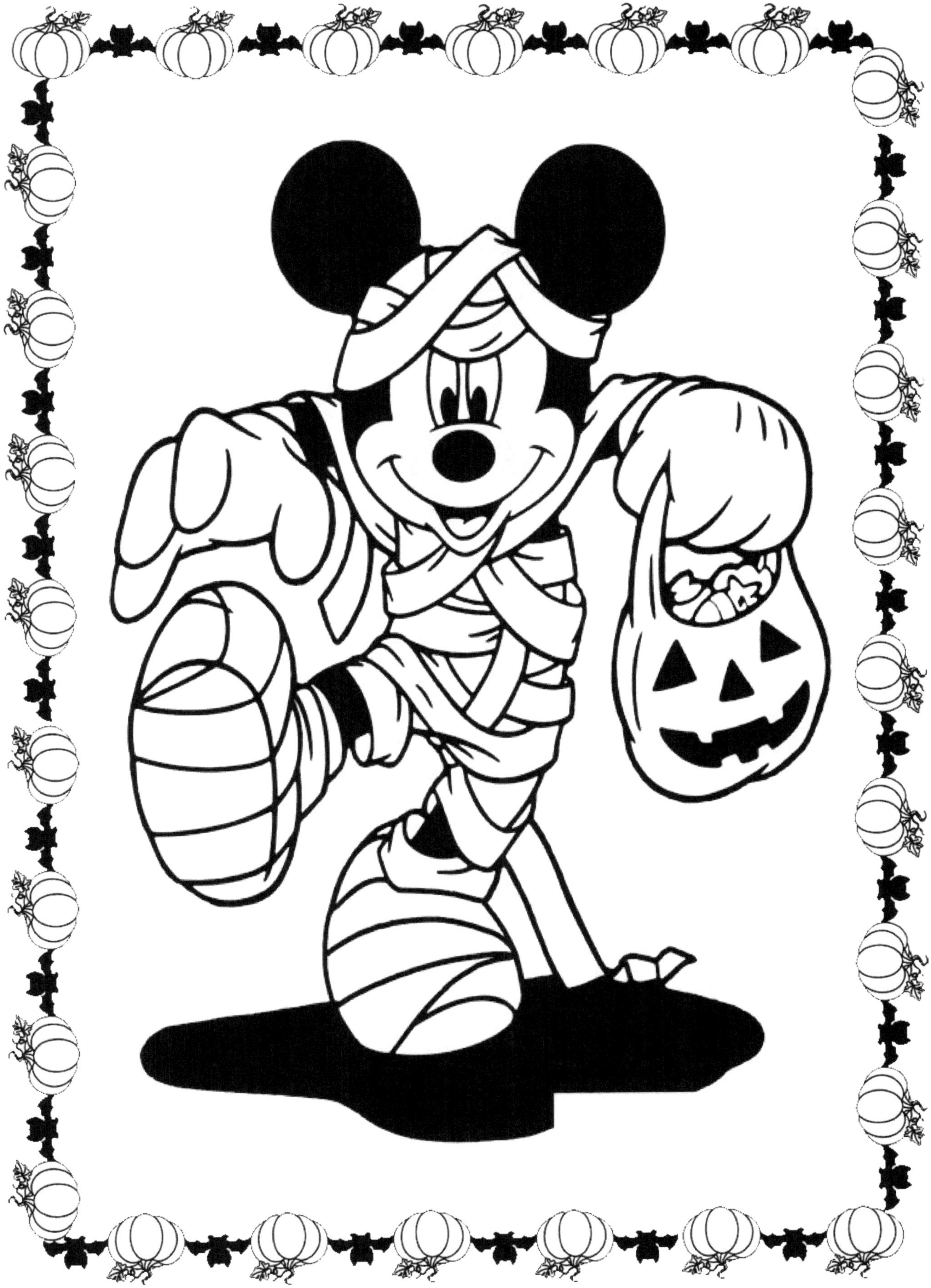

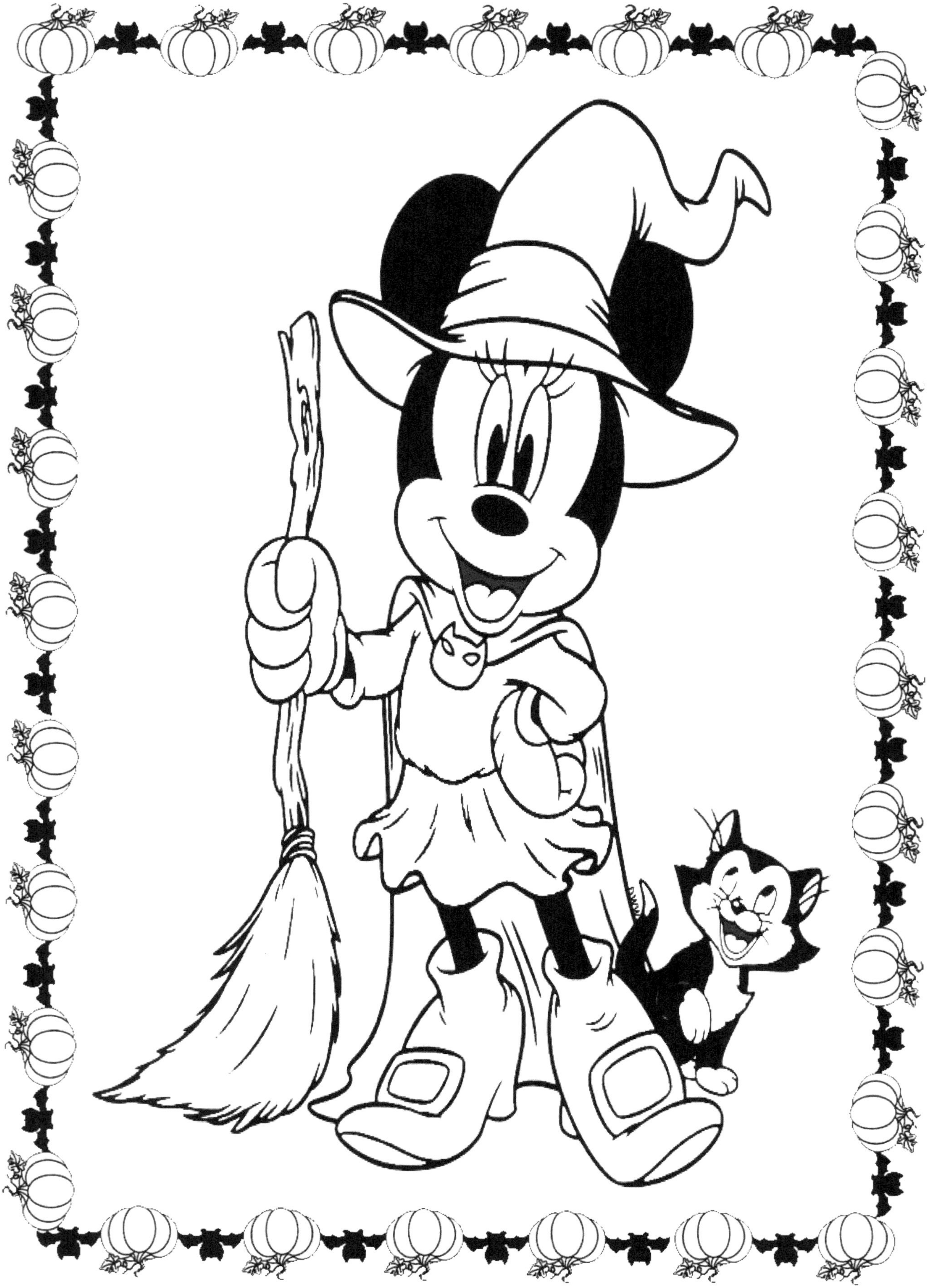

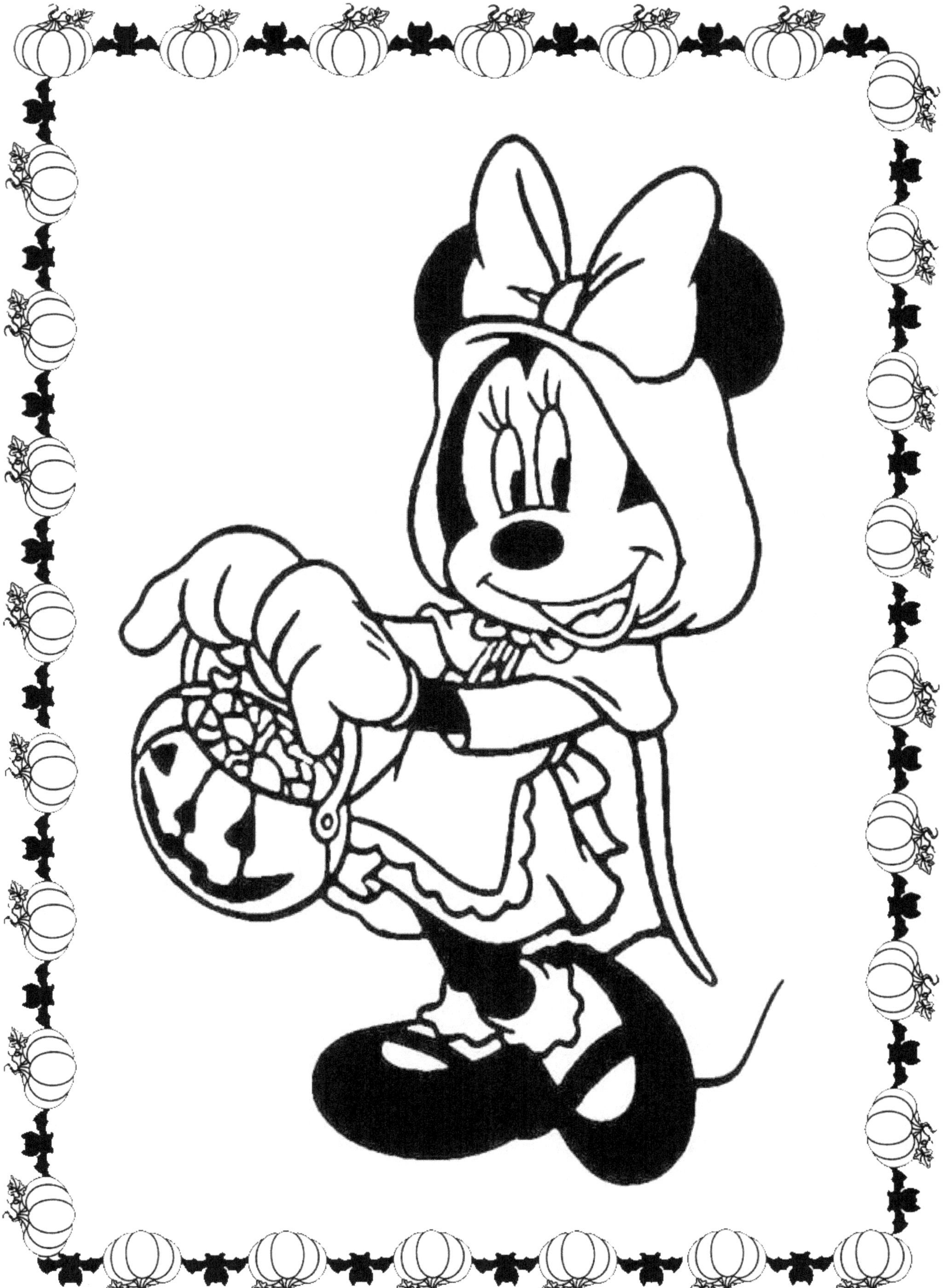

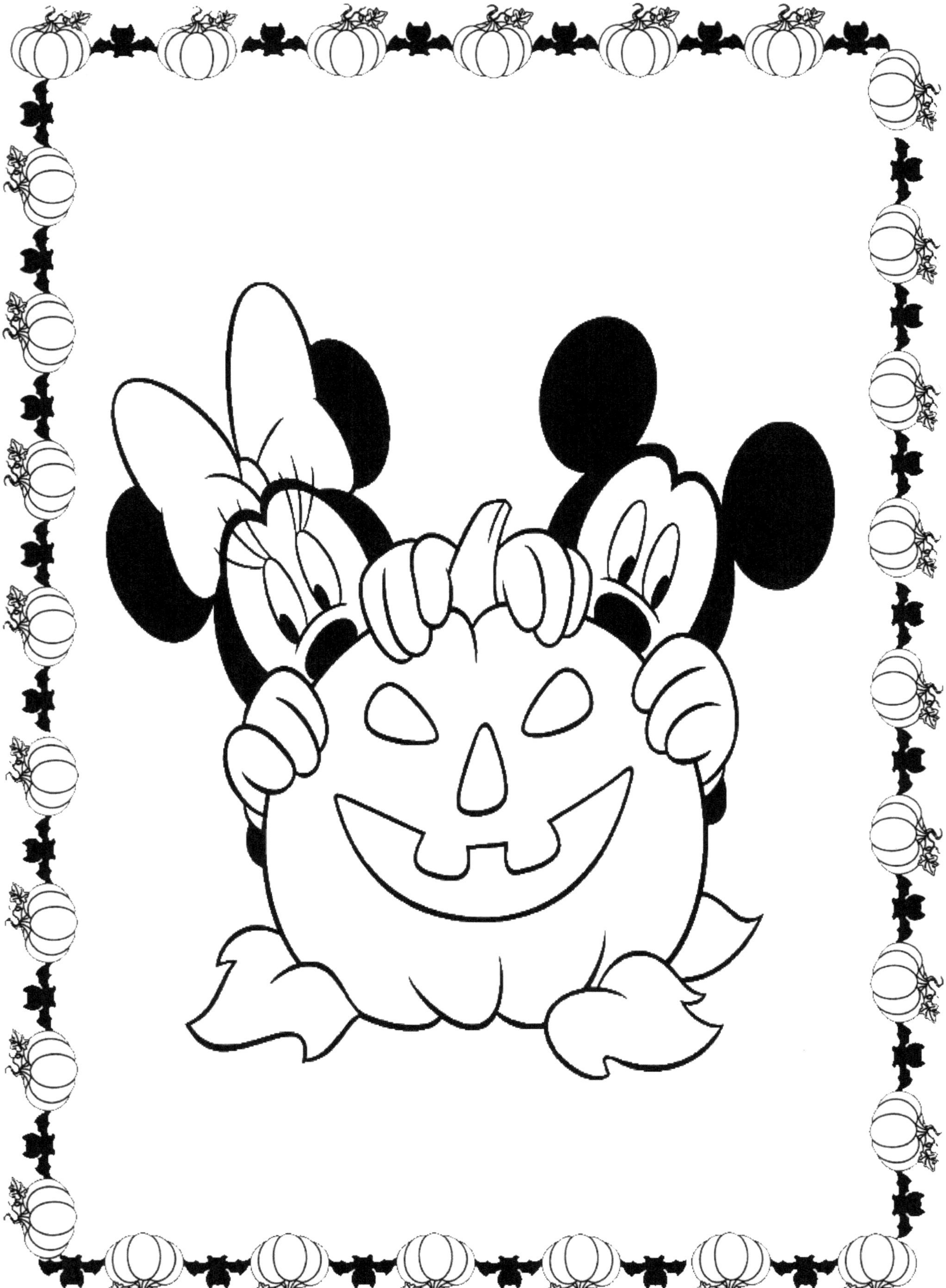

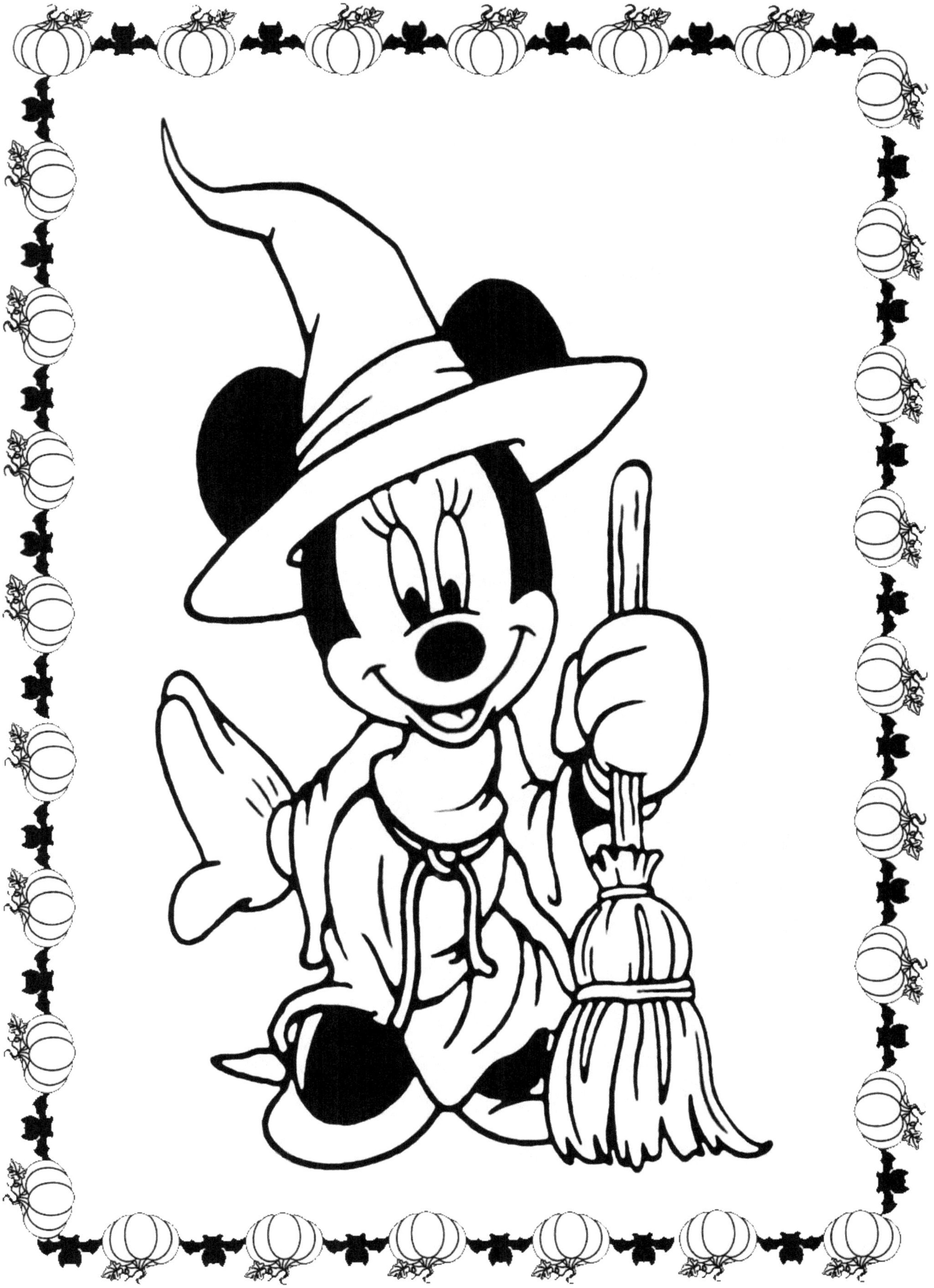

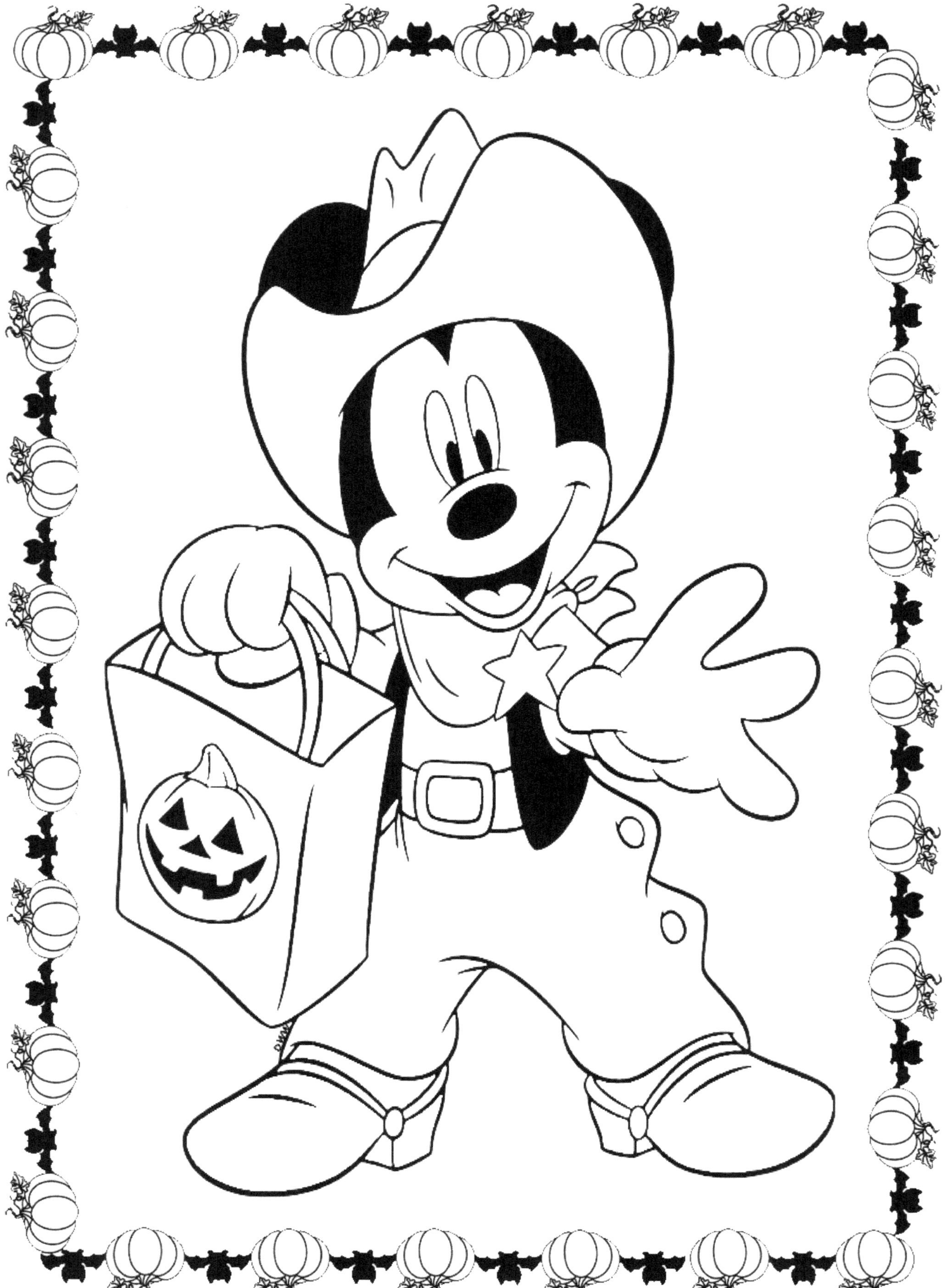

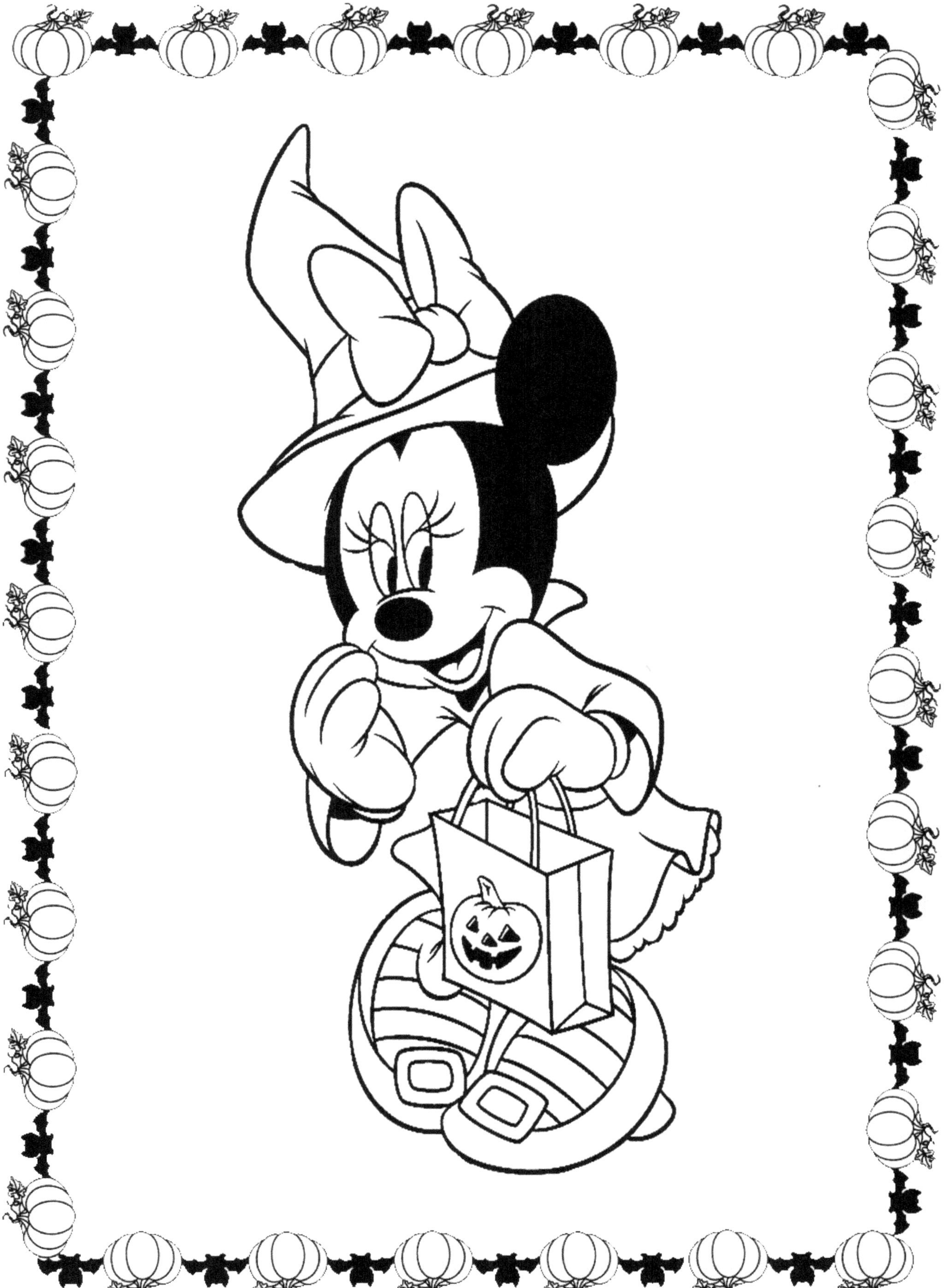

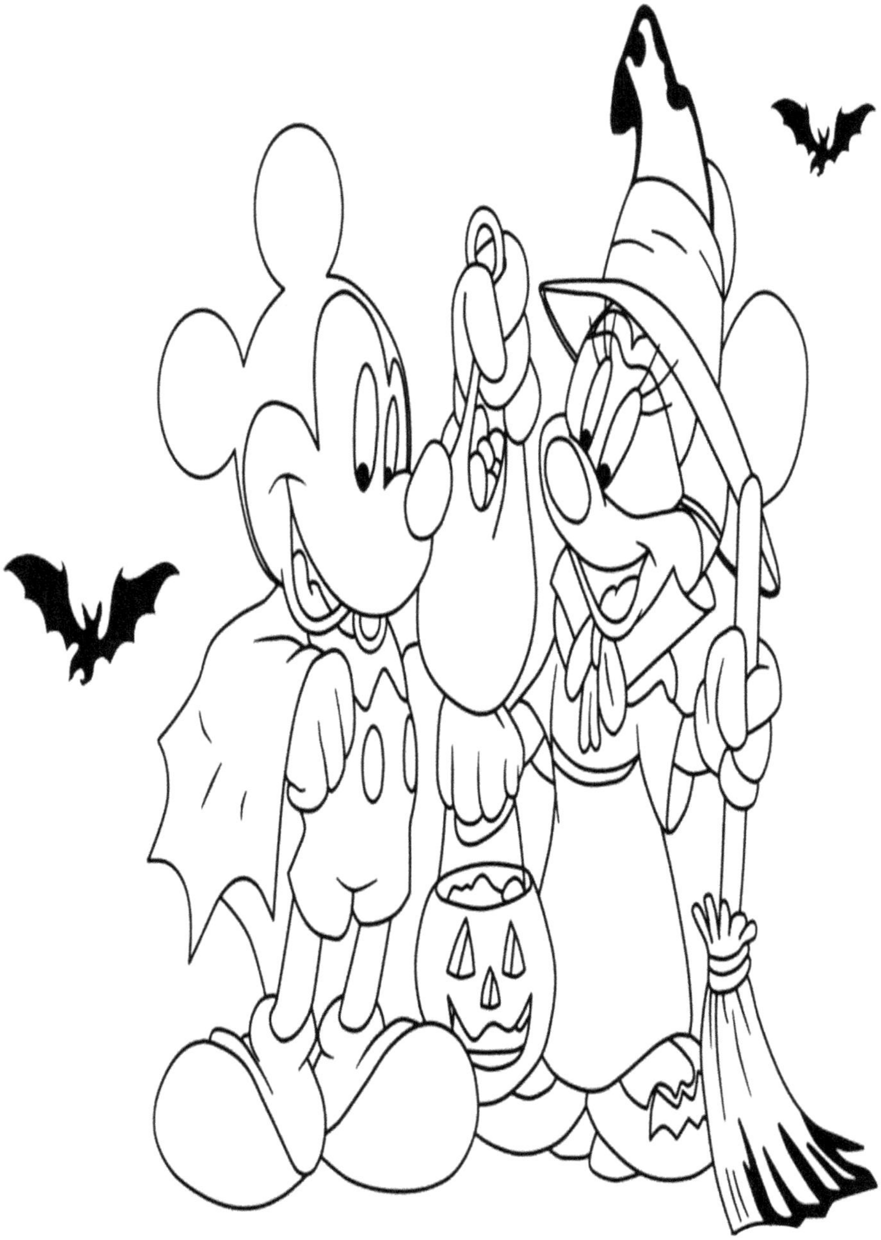

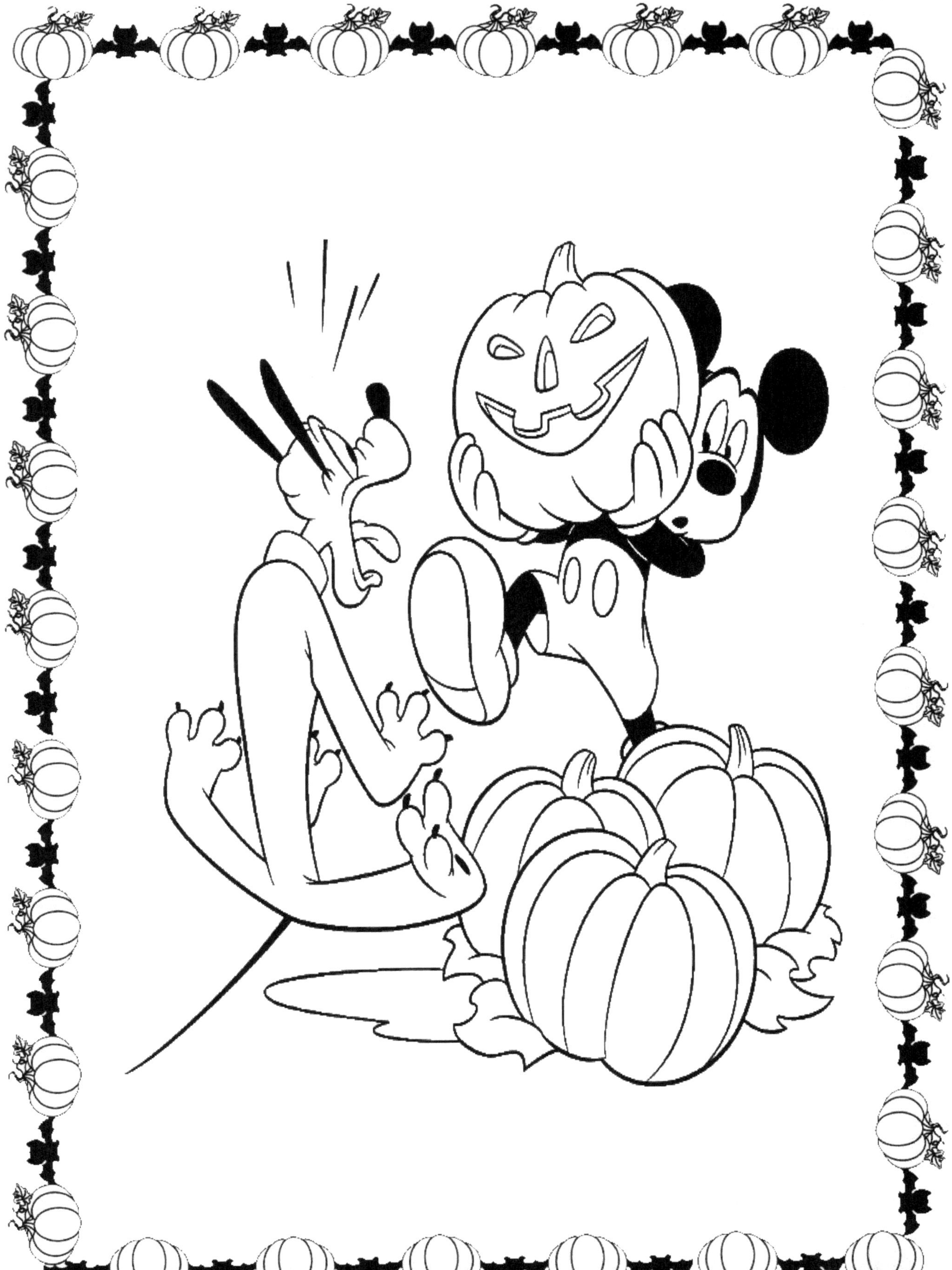

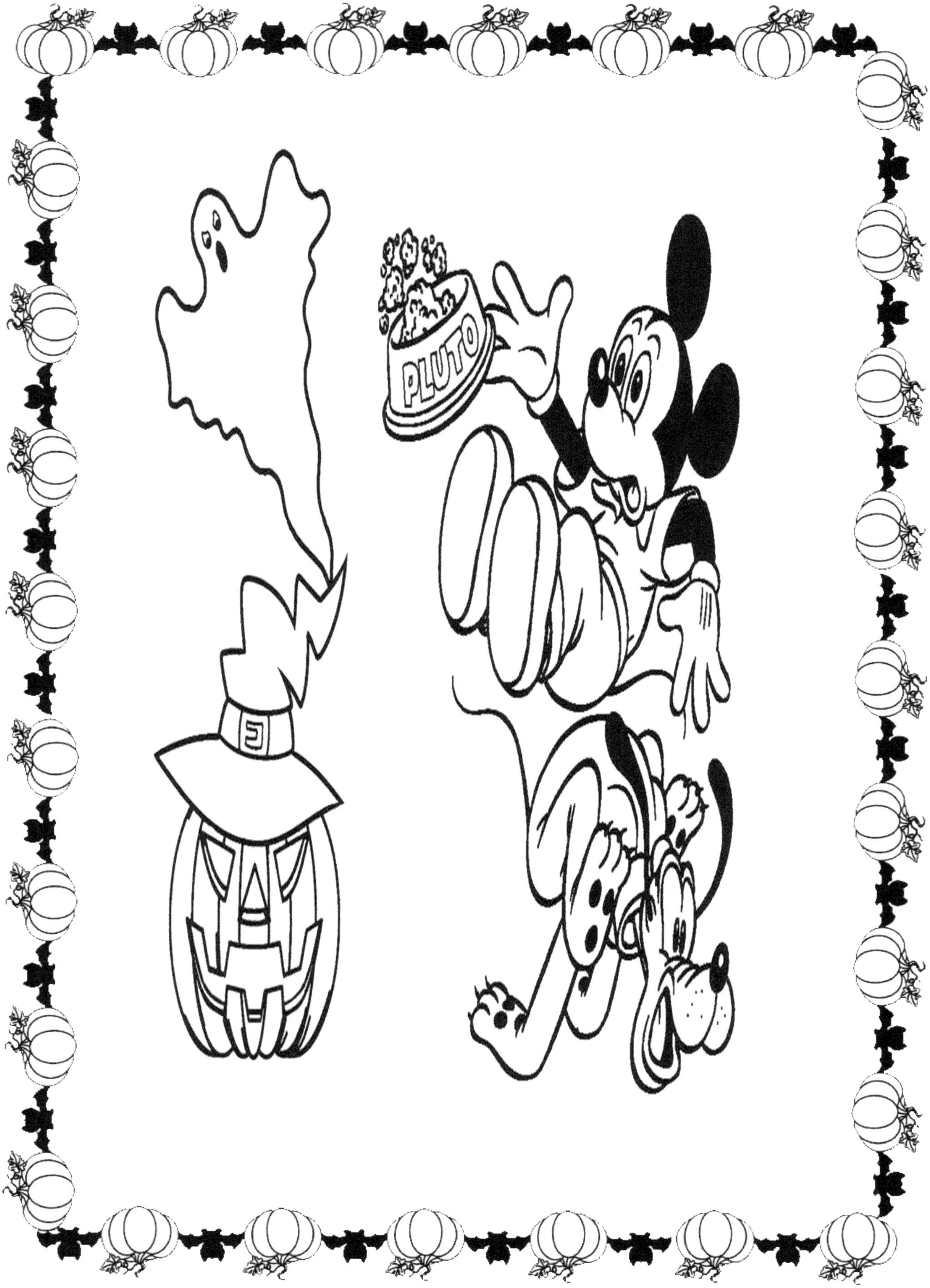
PLUTO

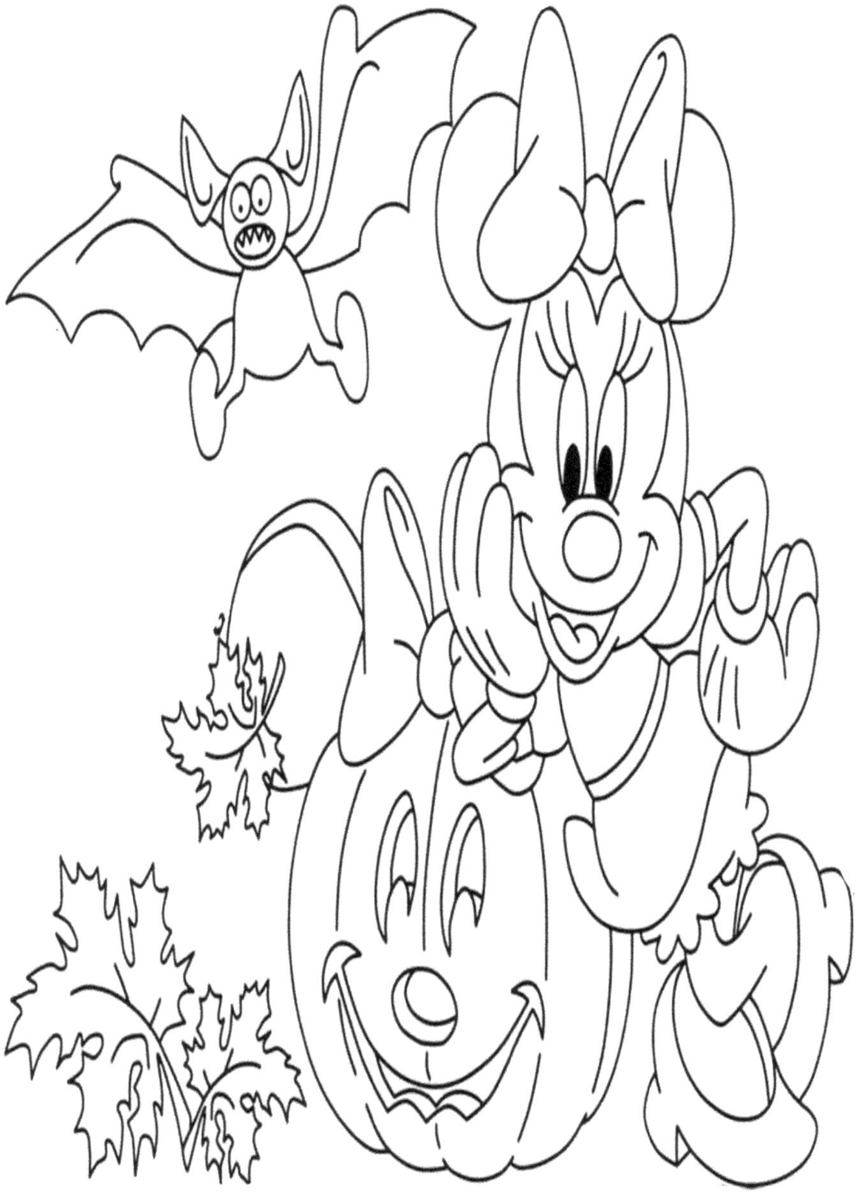

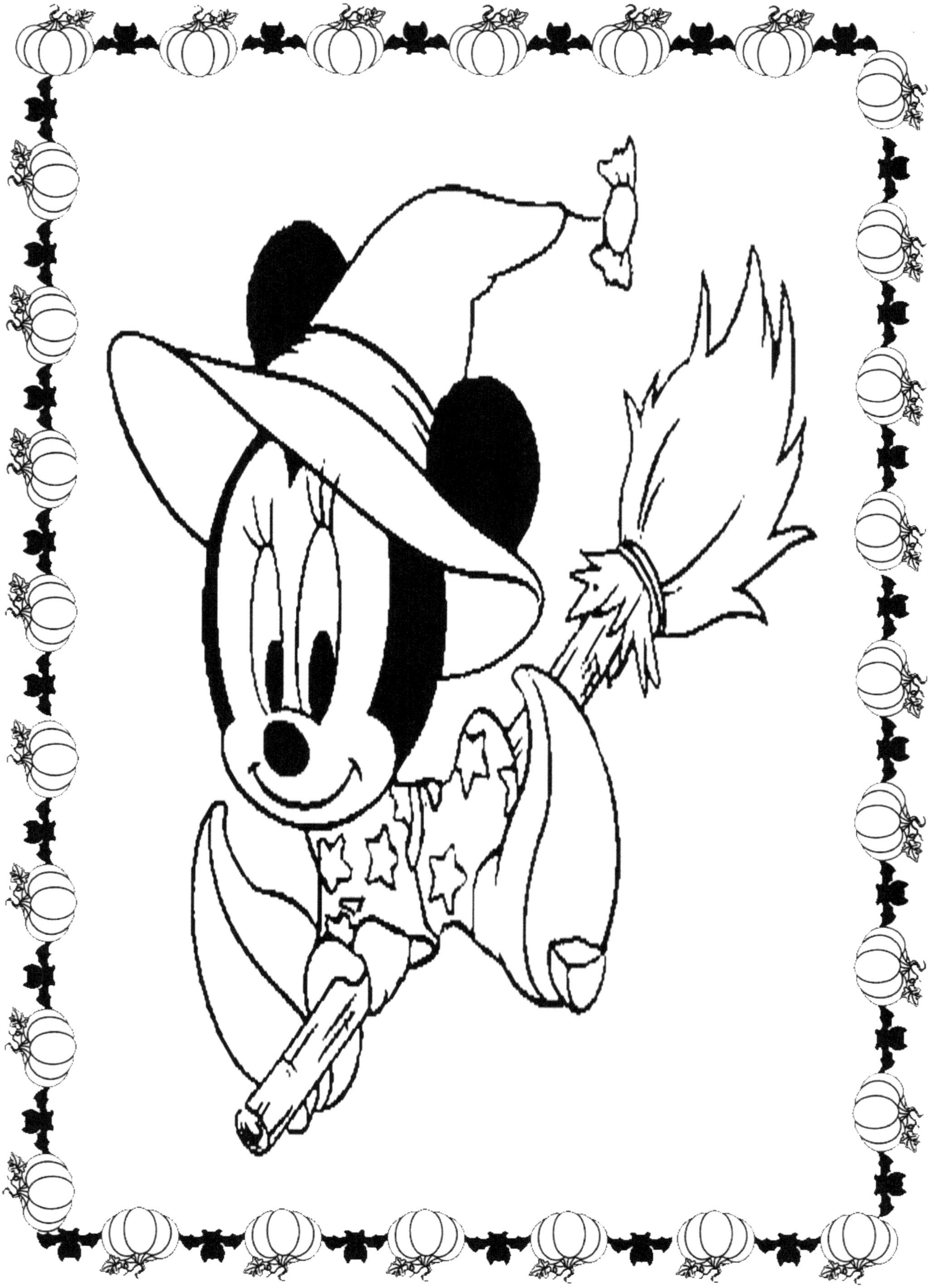

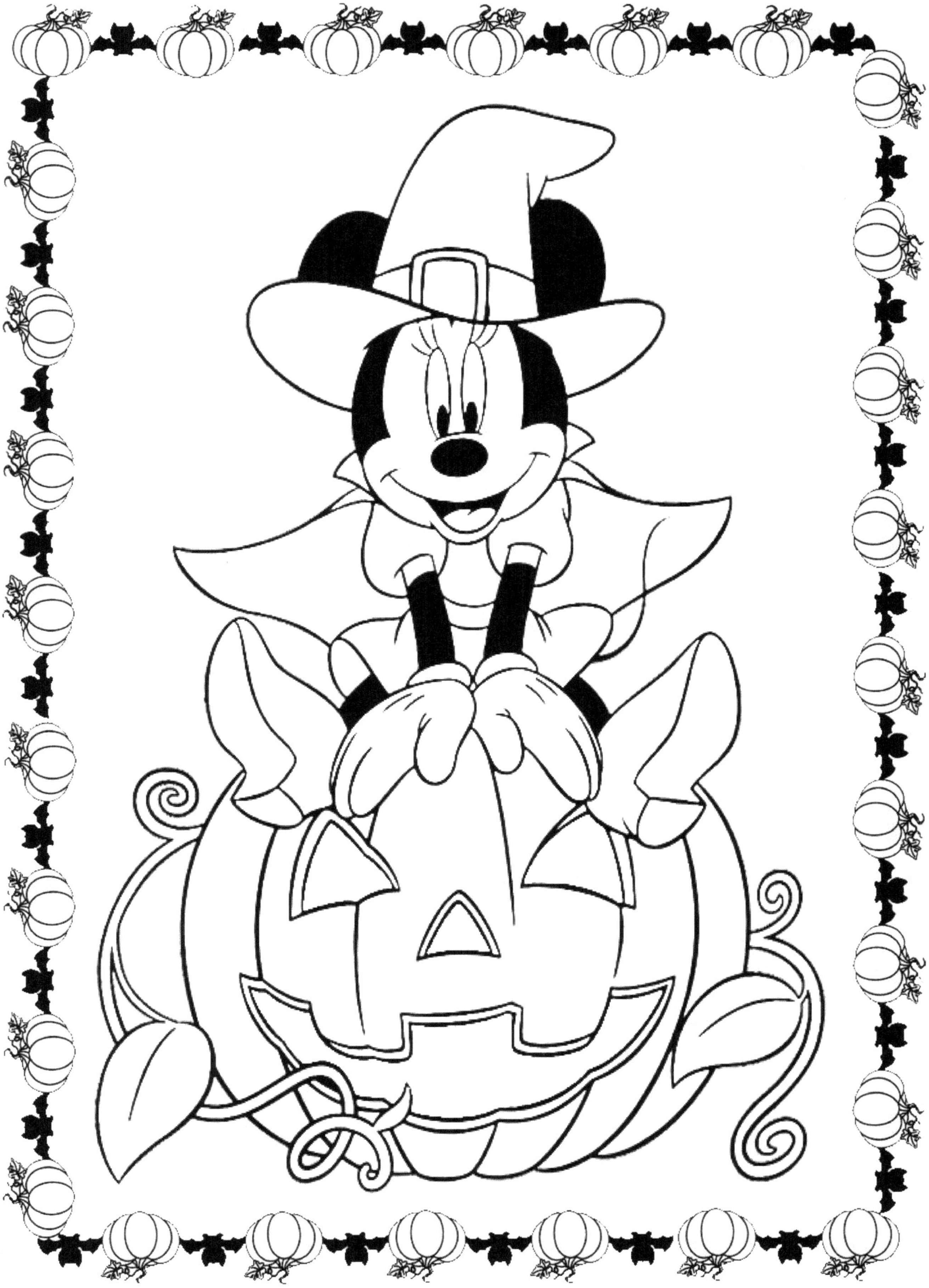

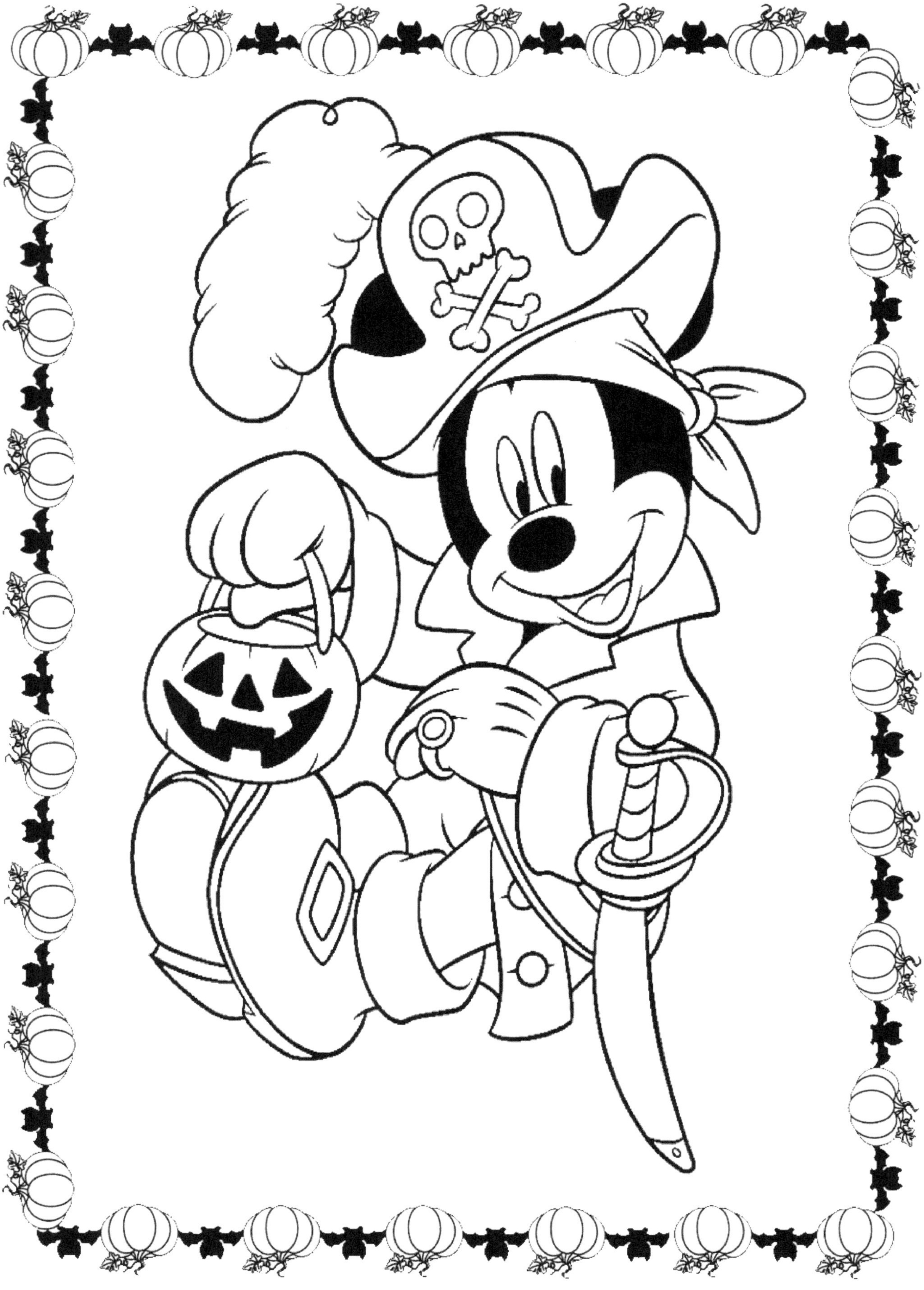

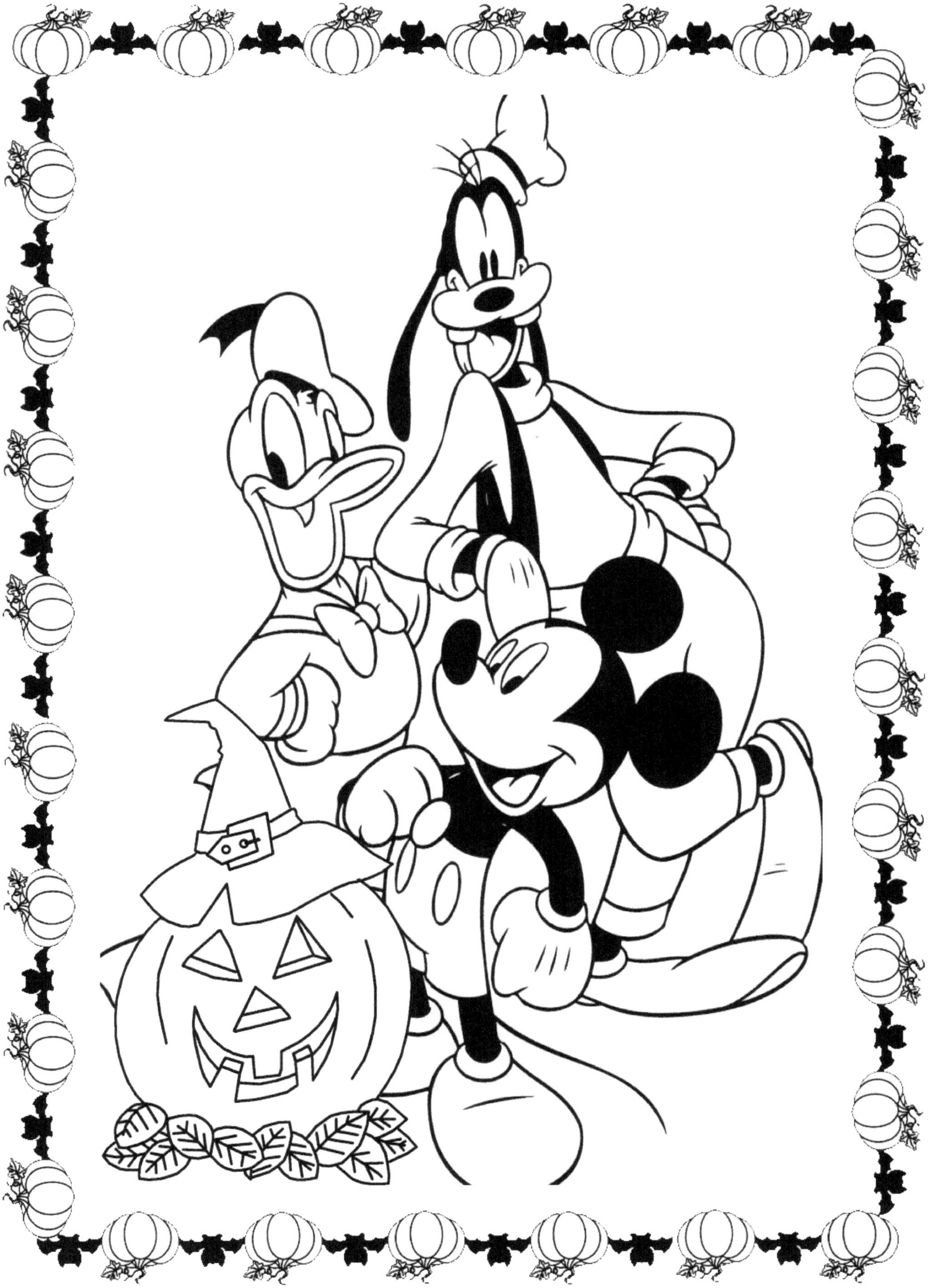

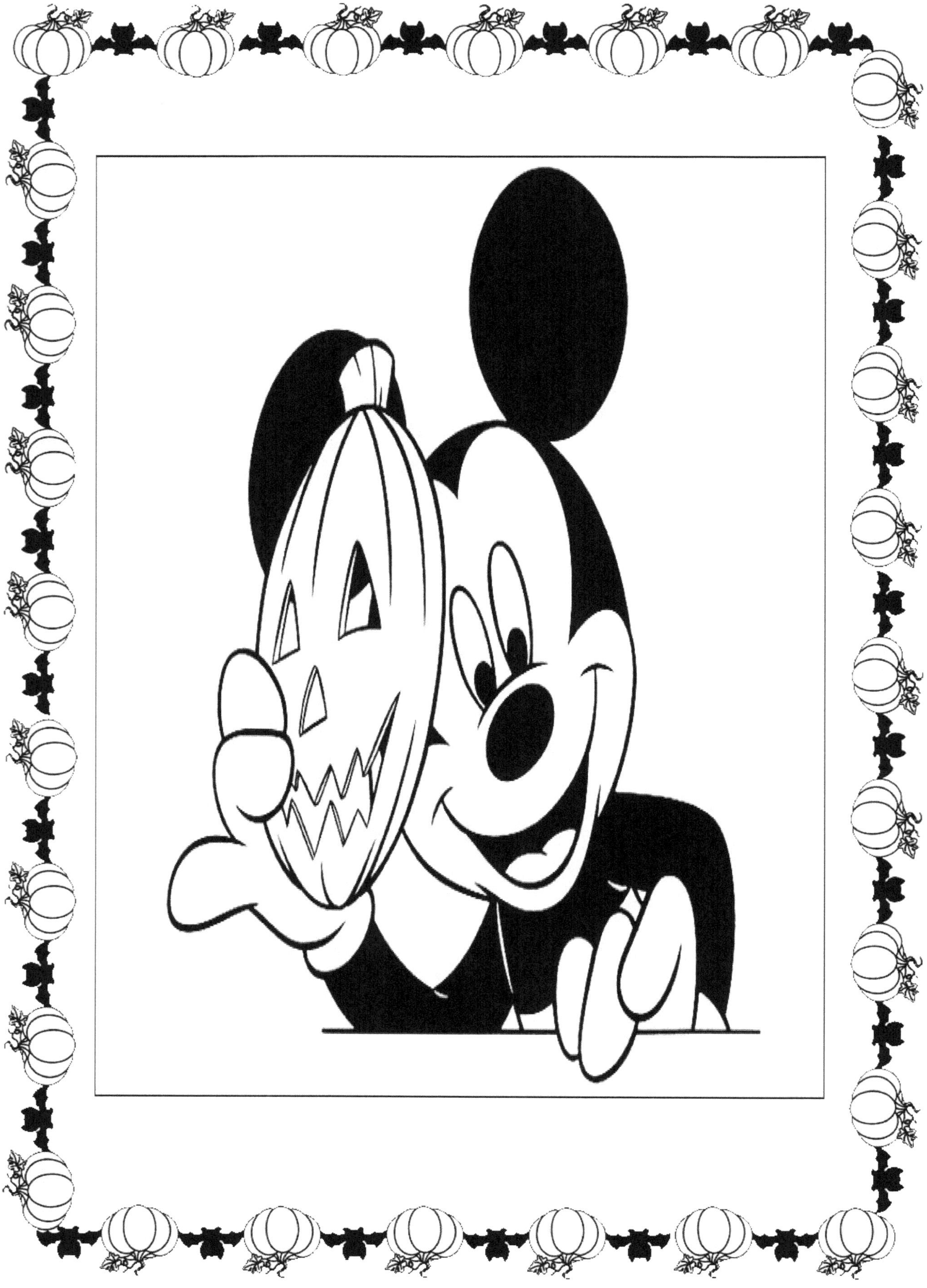

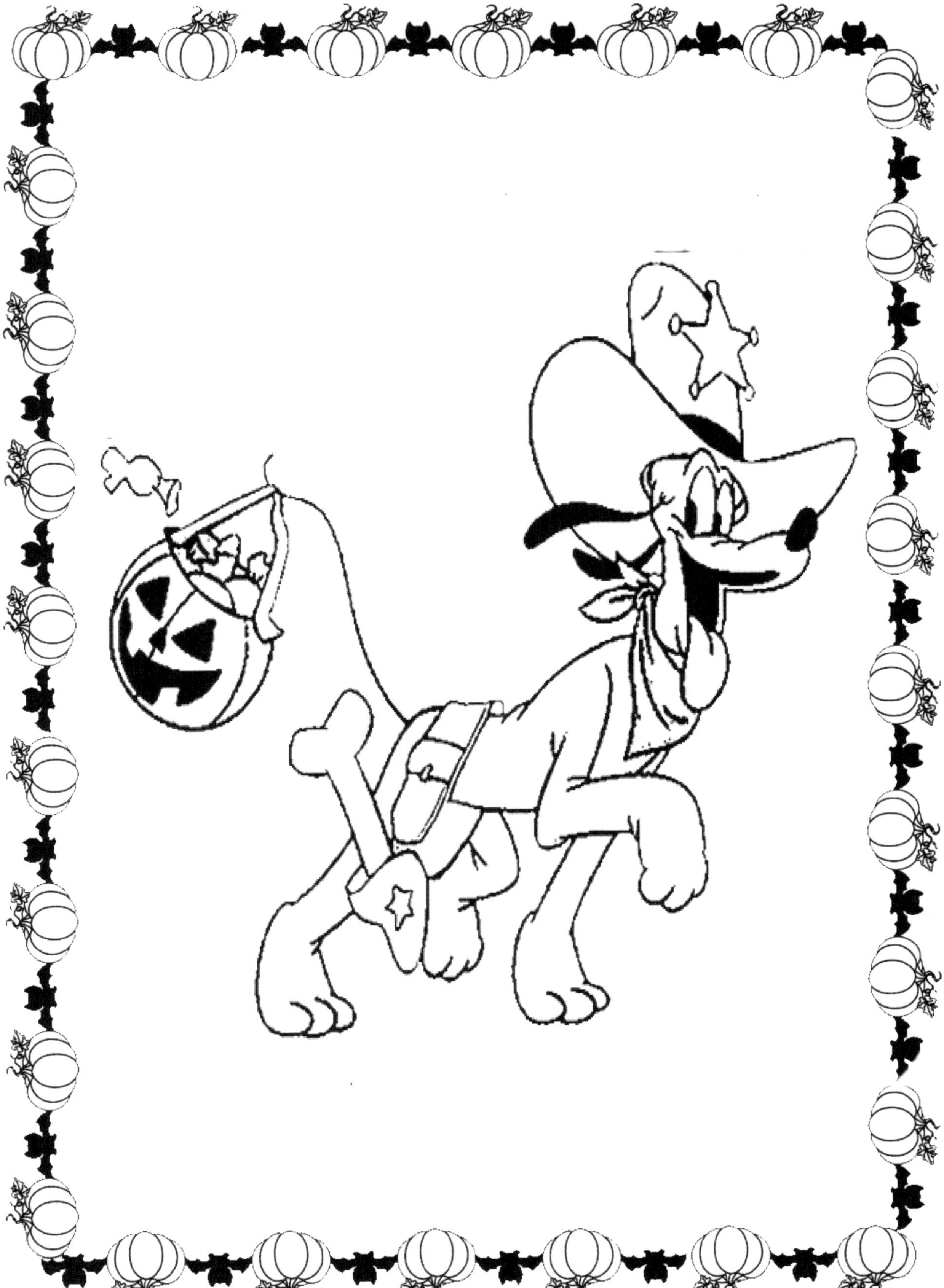

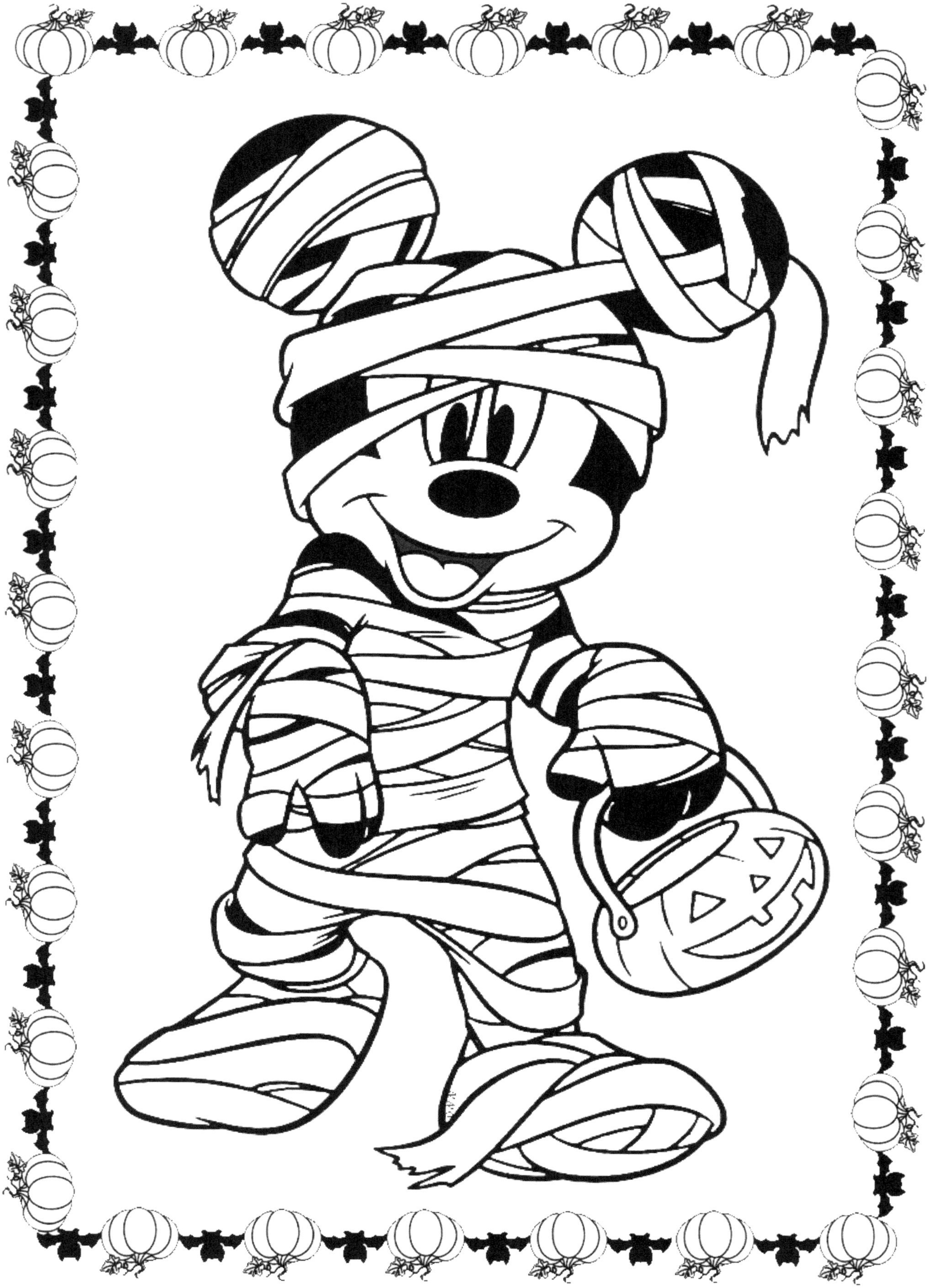

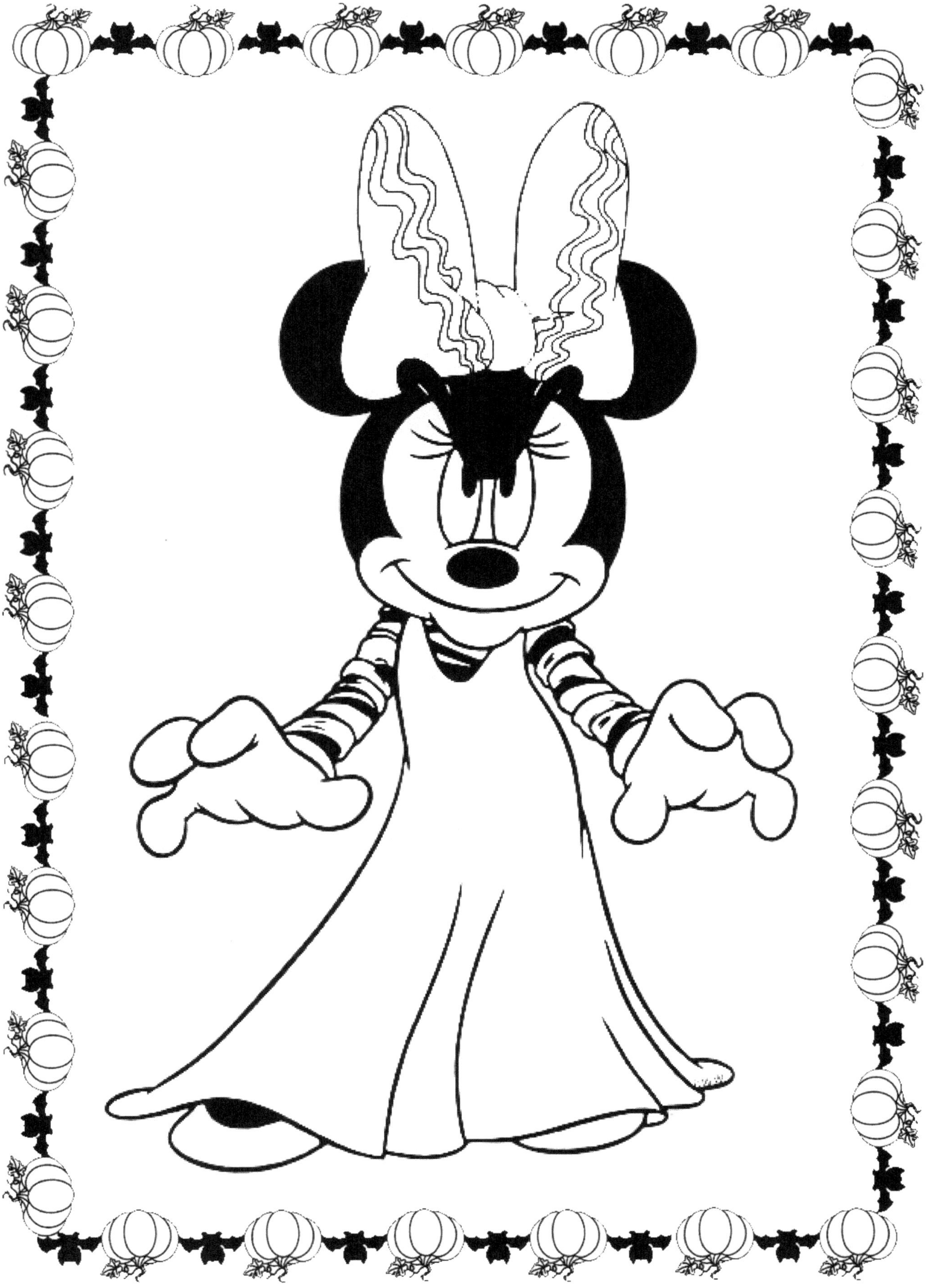

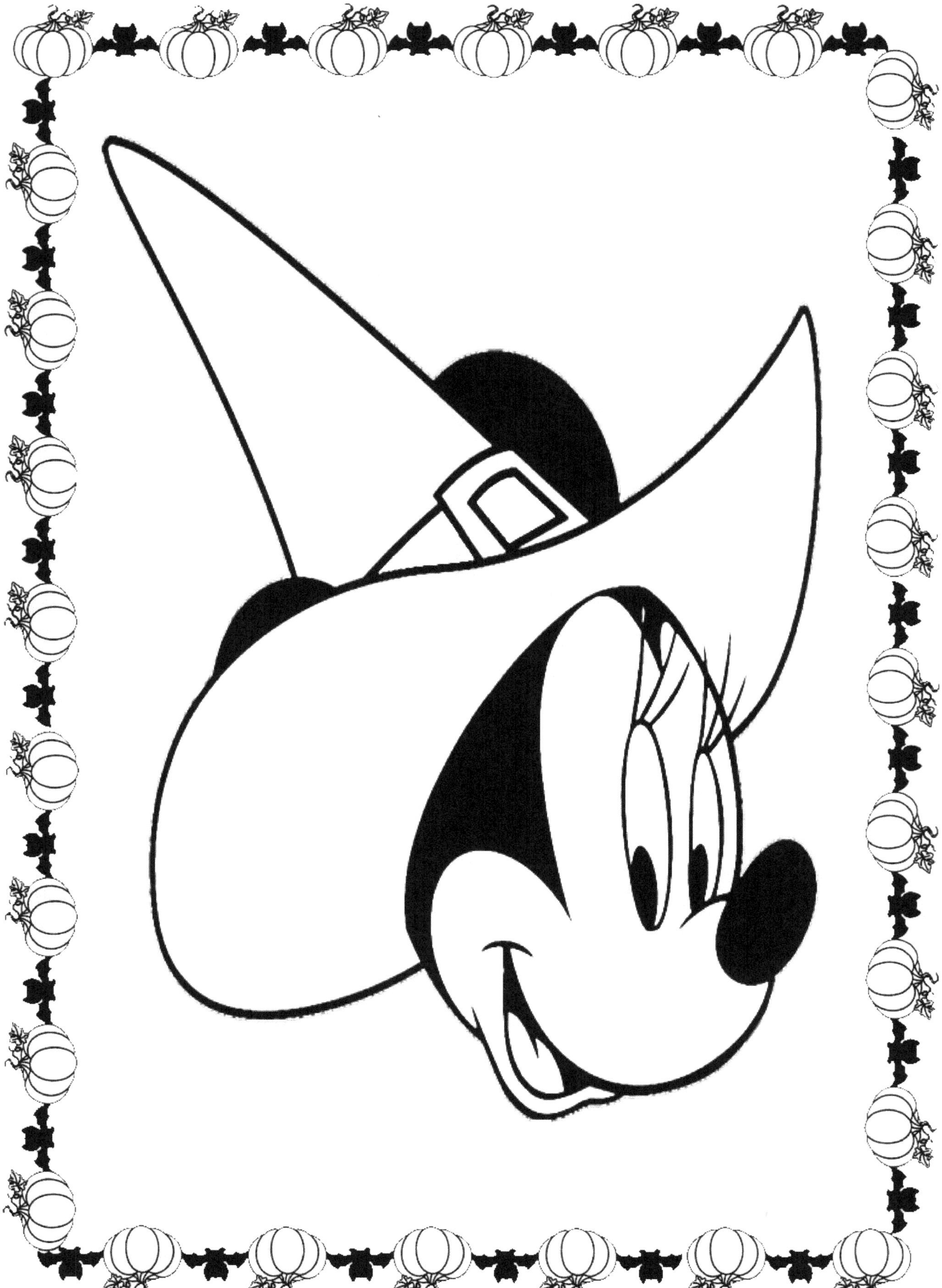

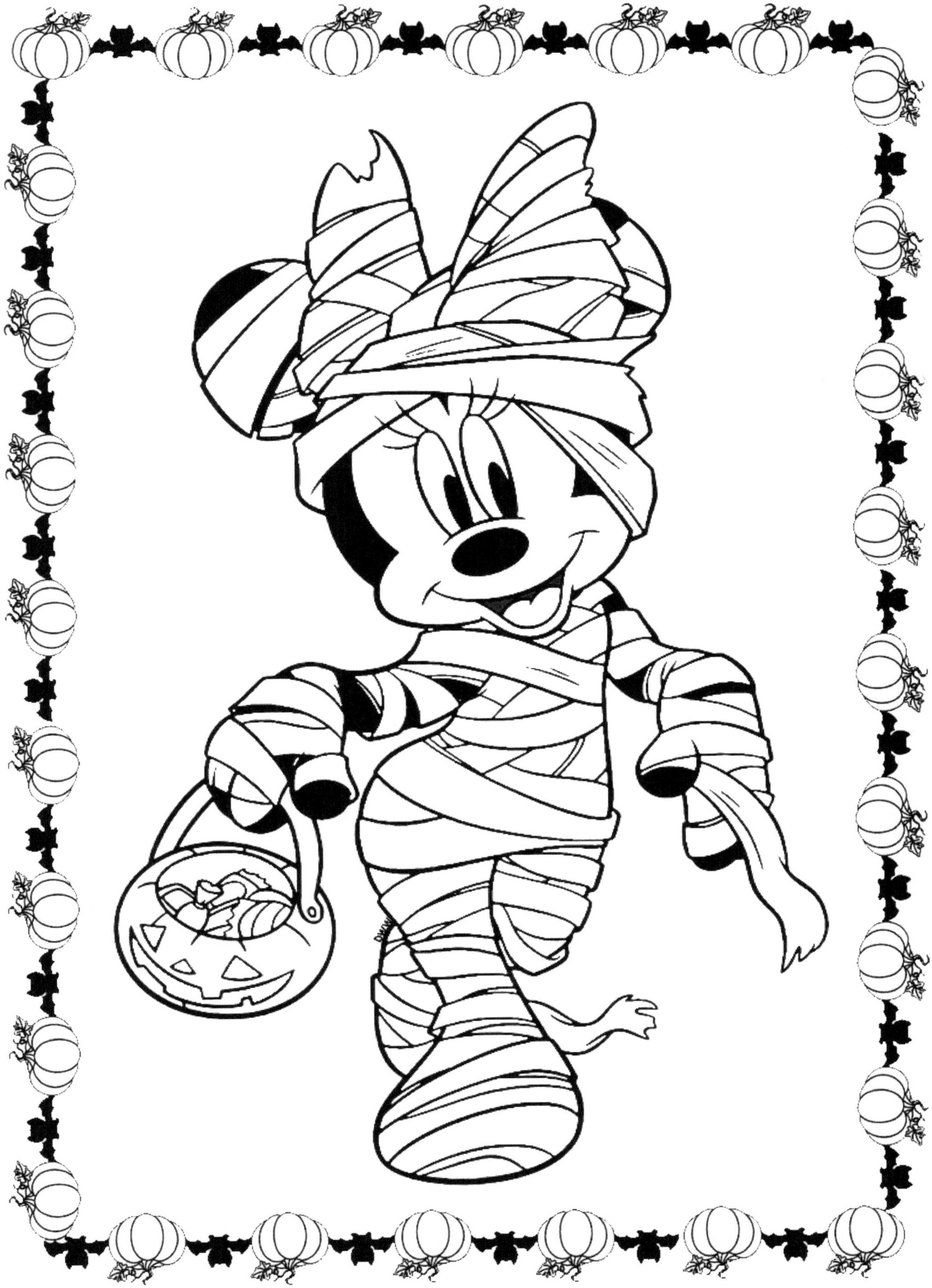

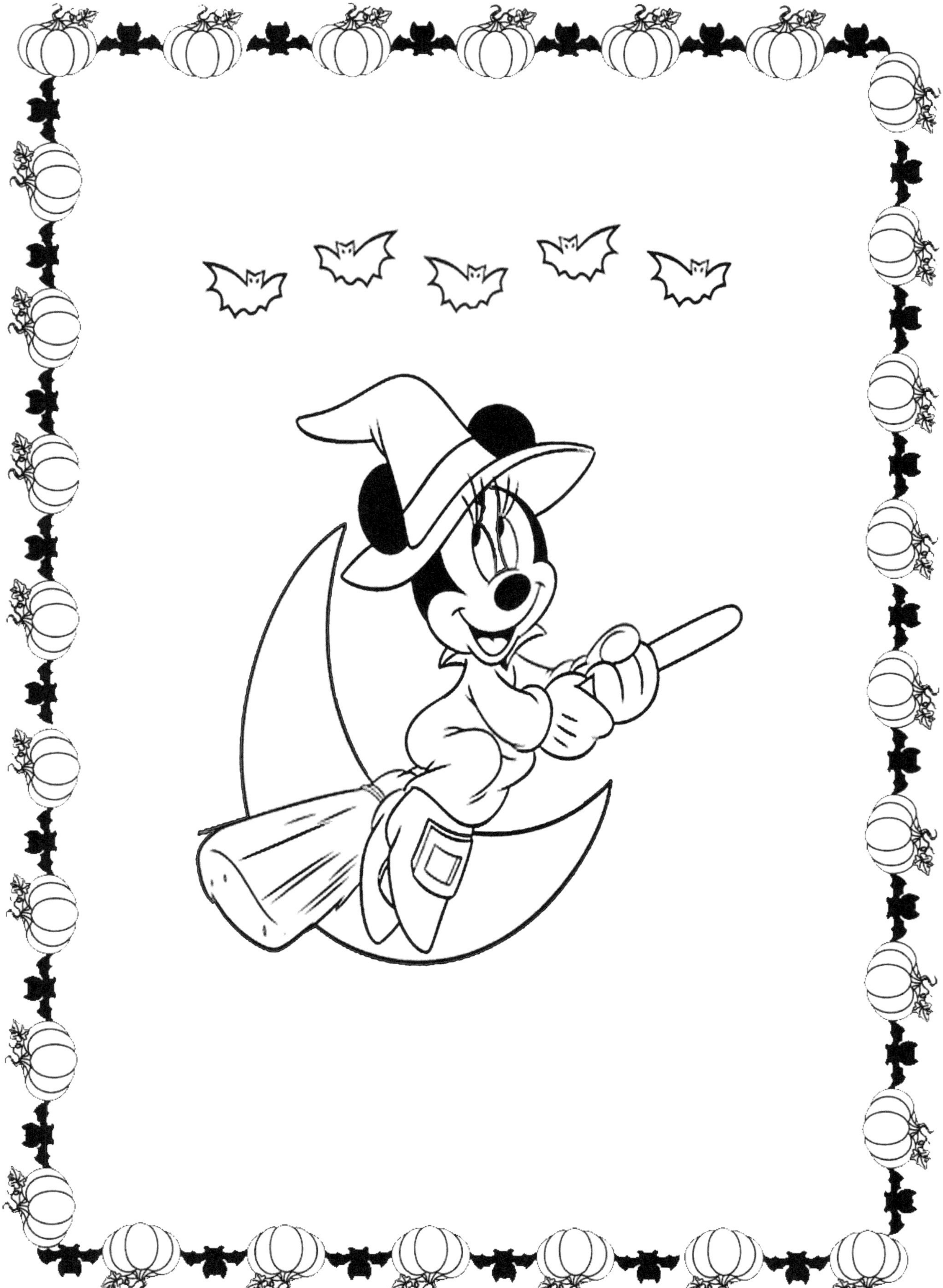

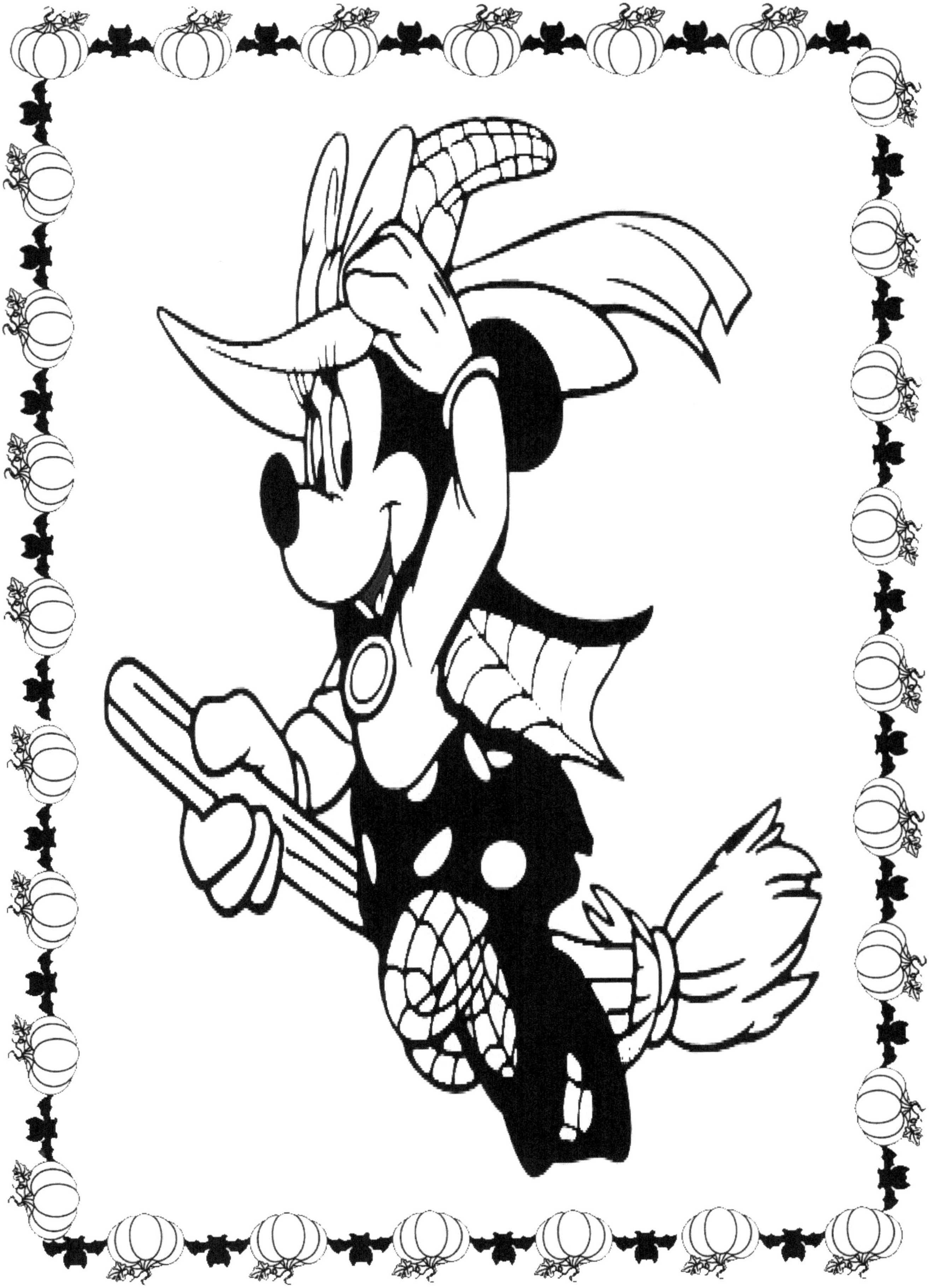

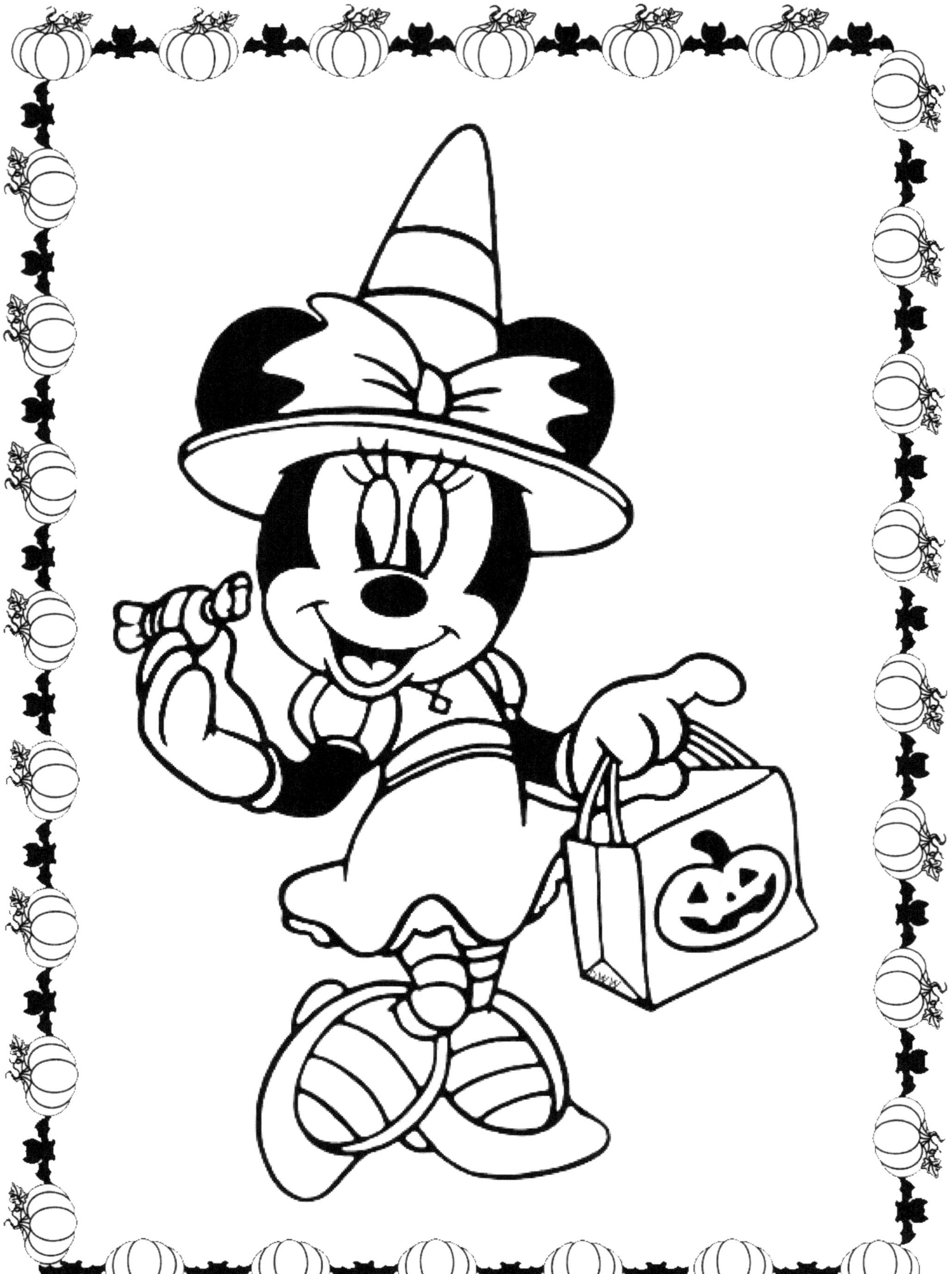

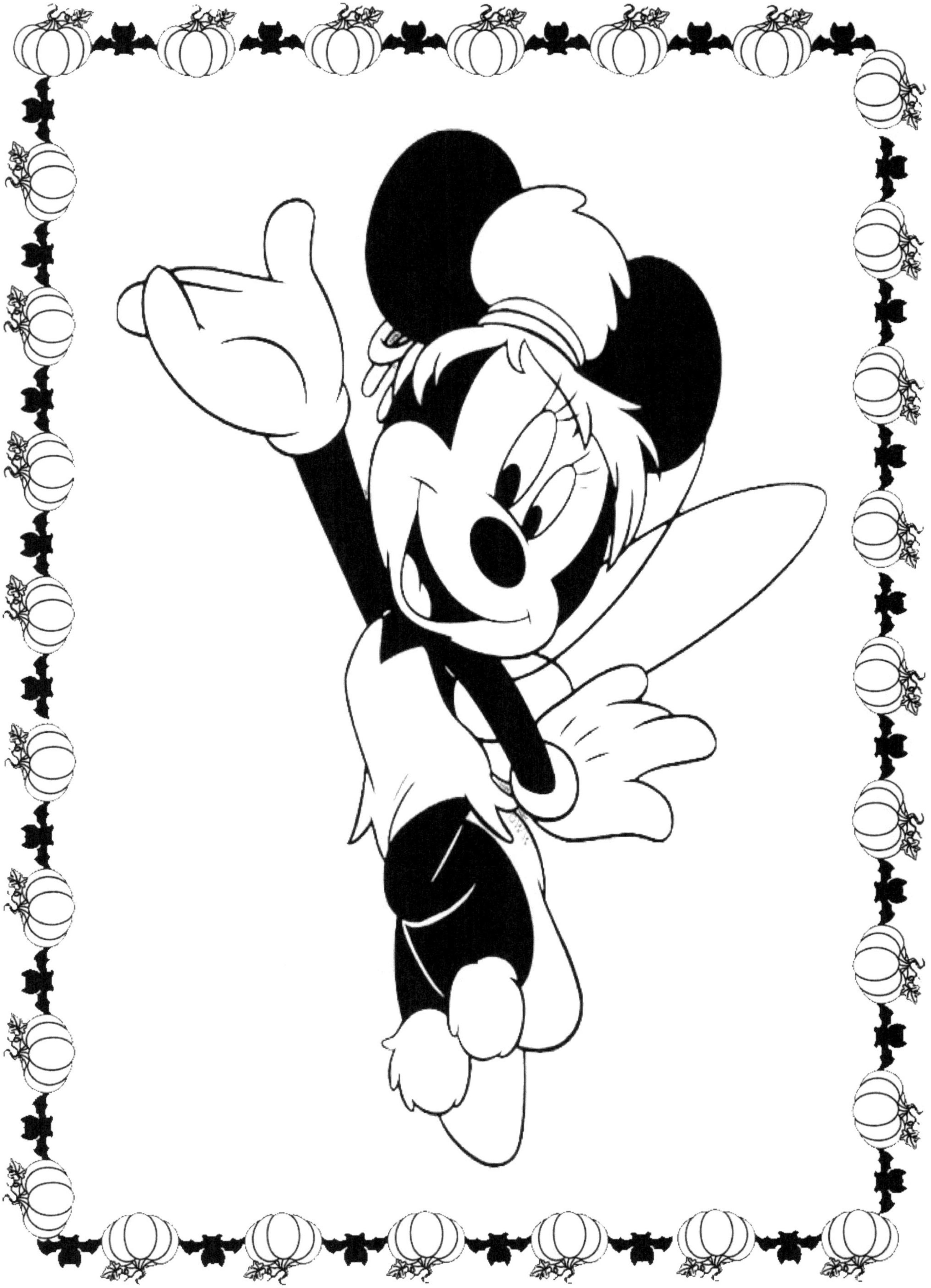

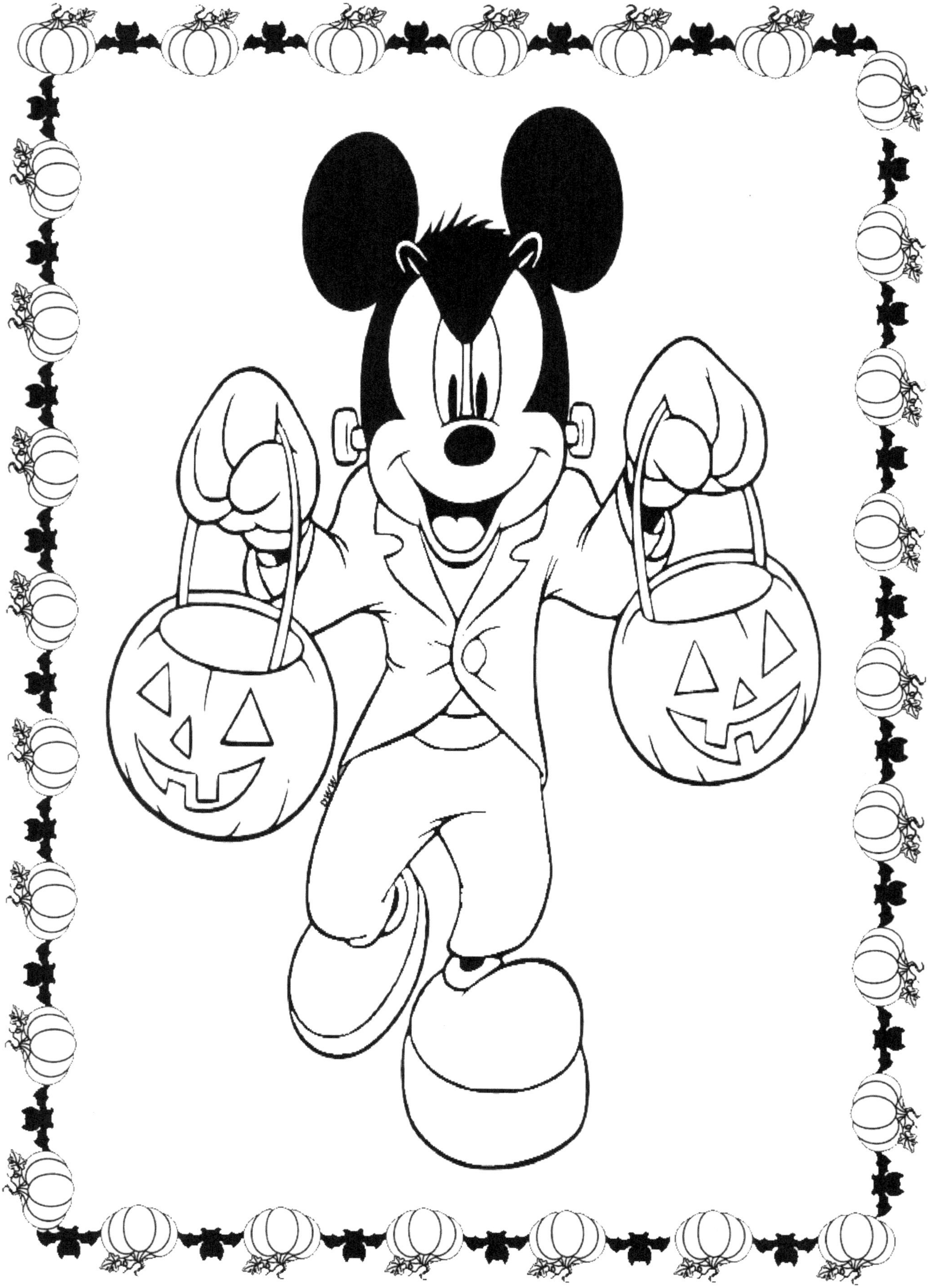

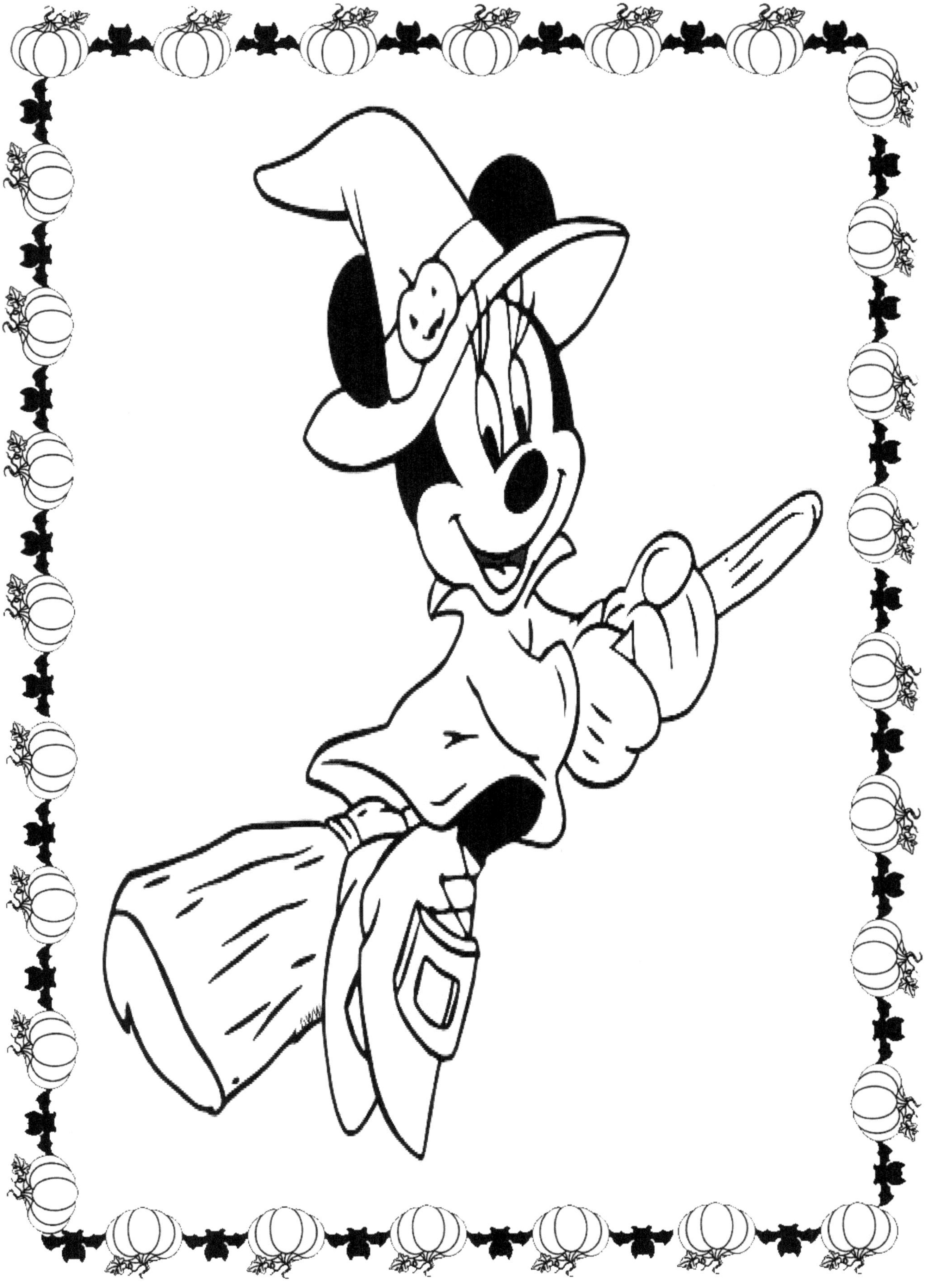

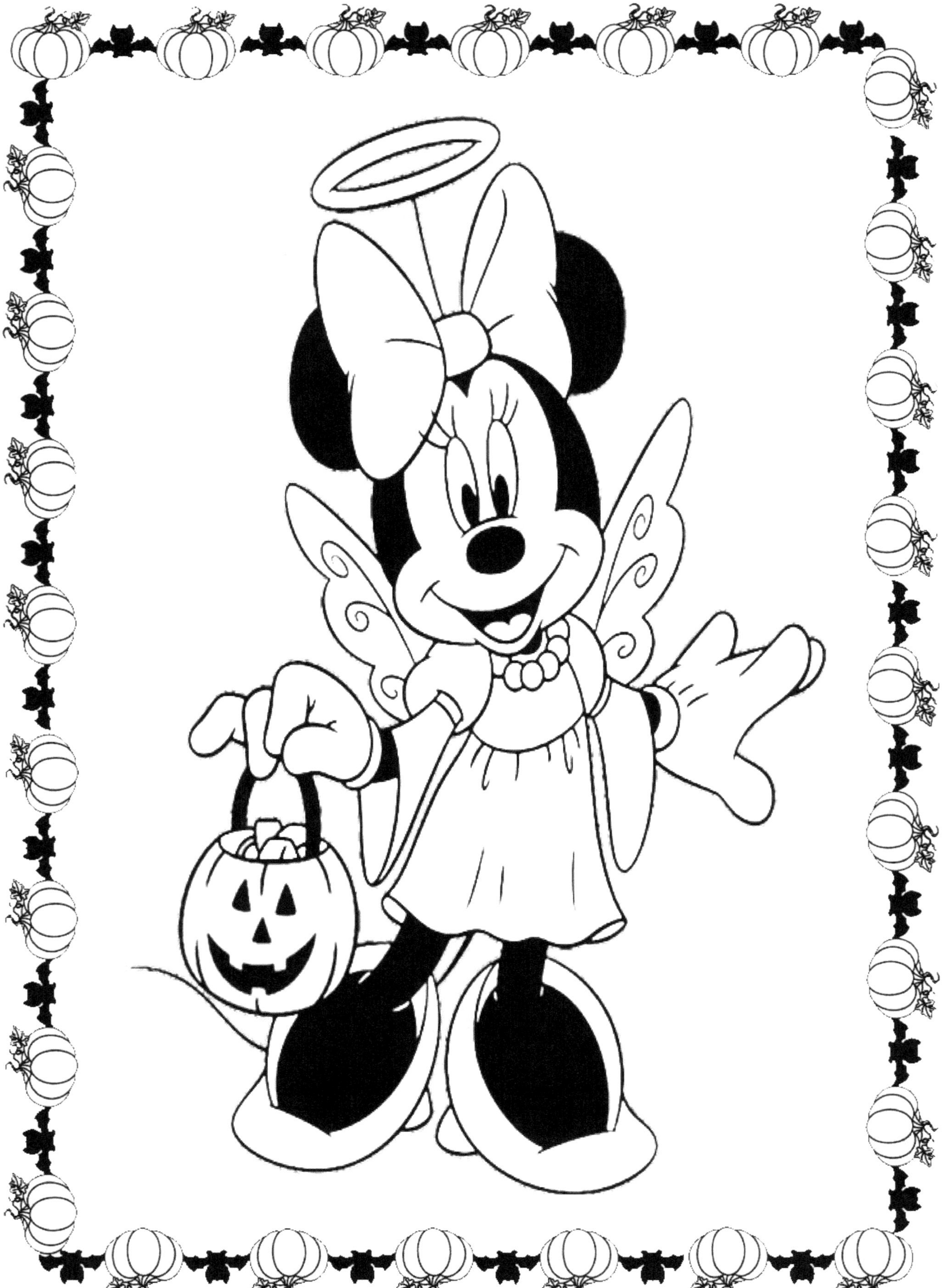

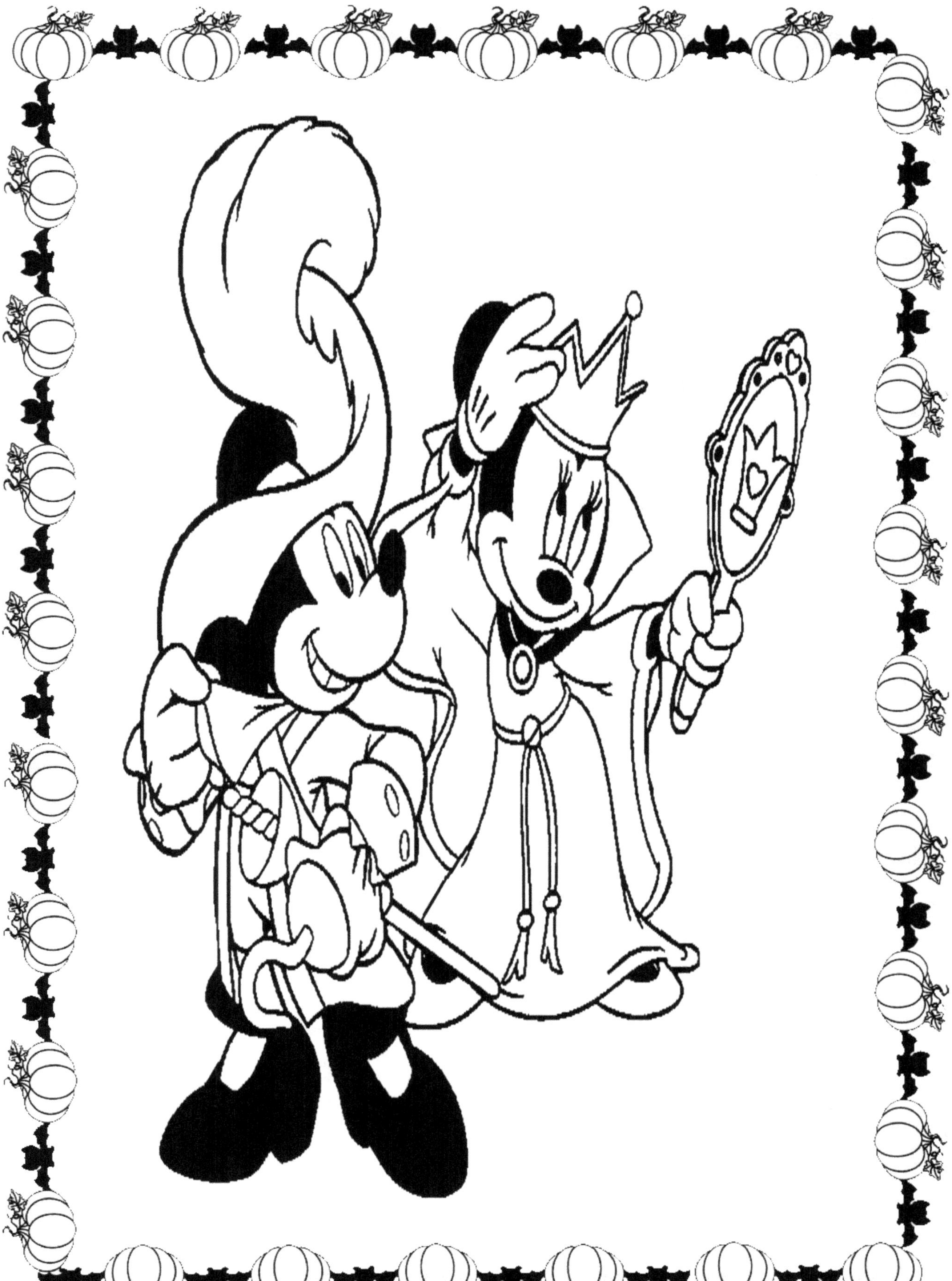

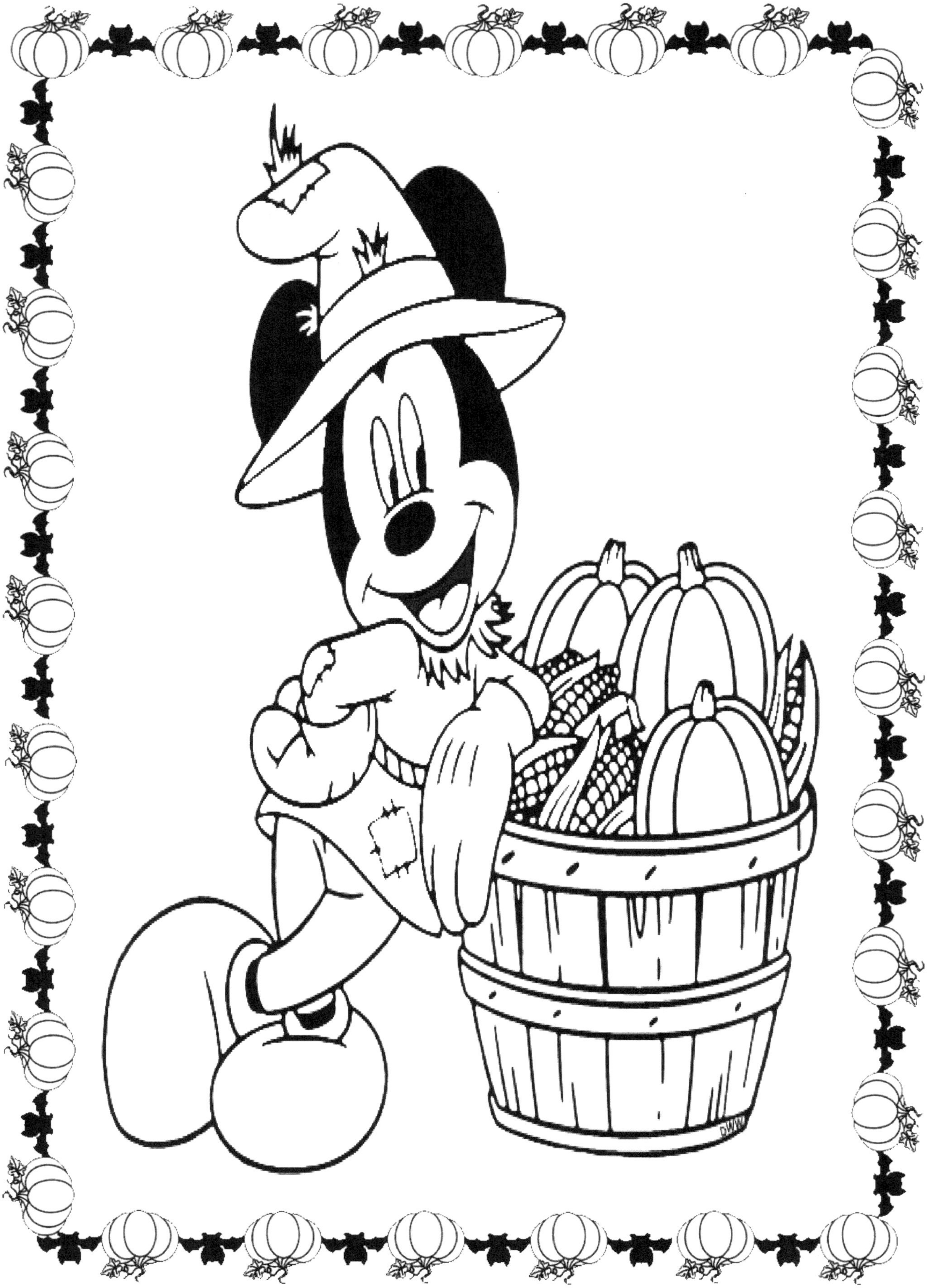

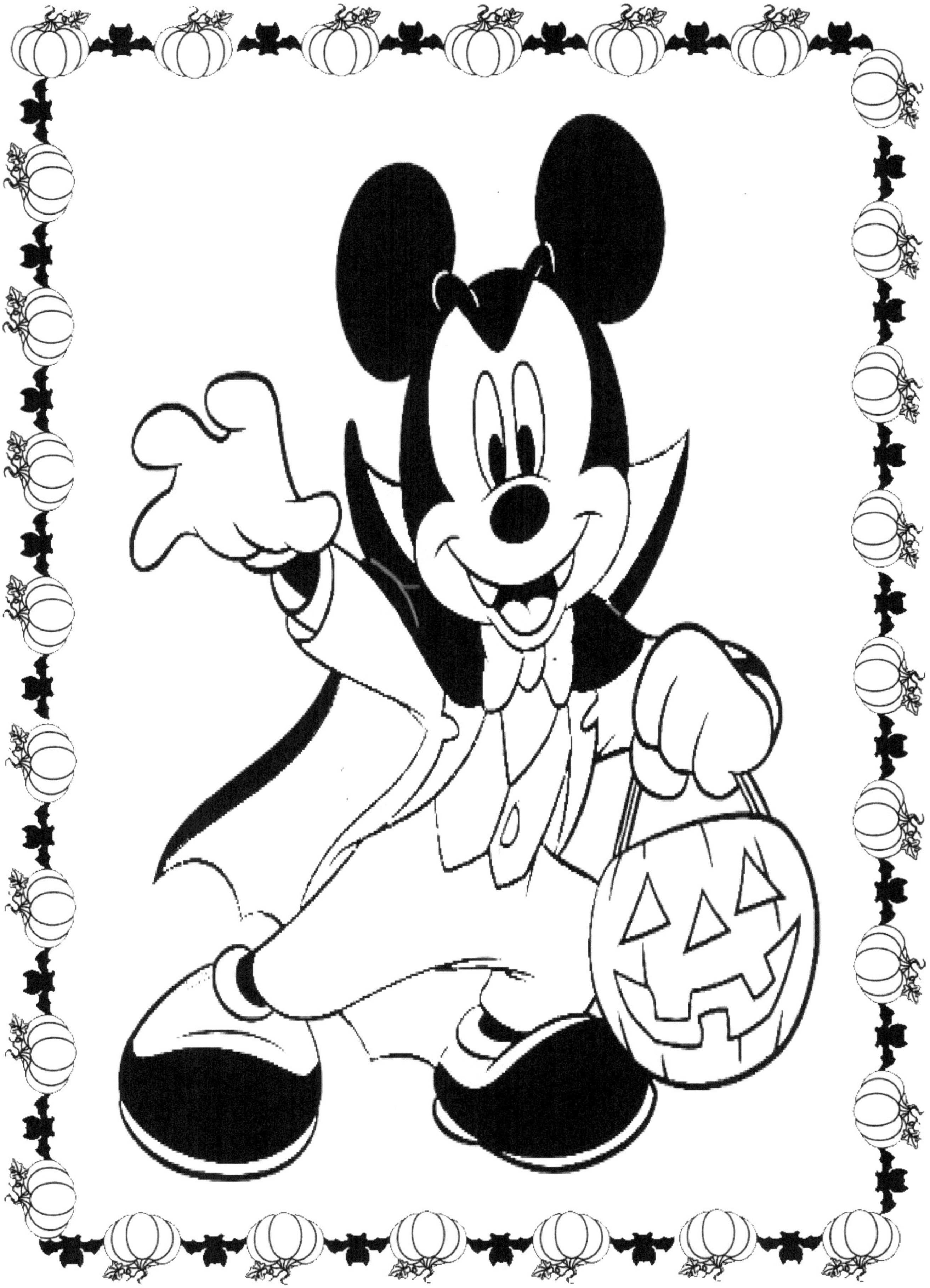

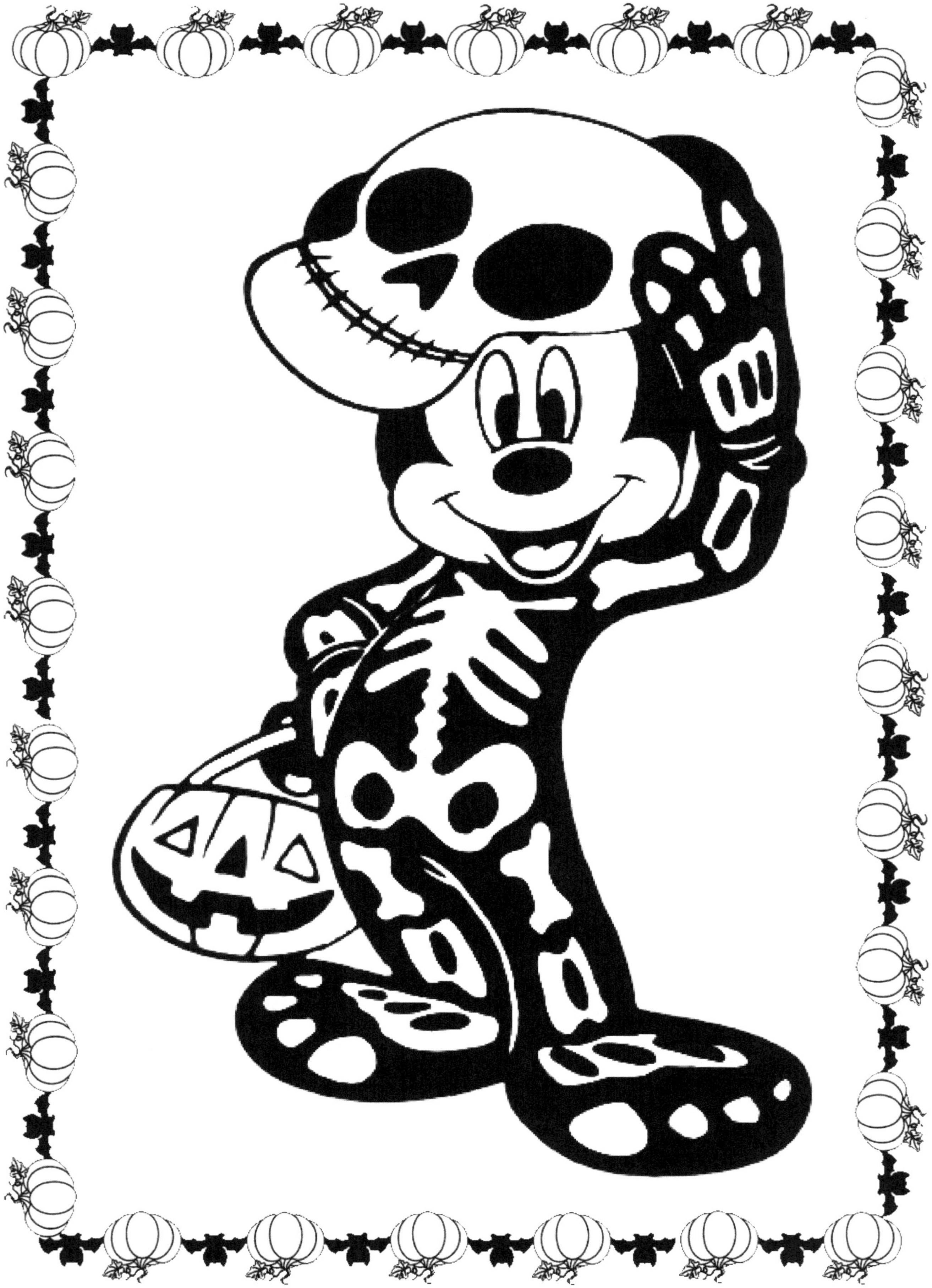

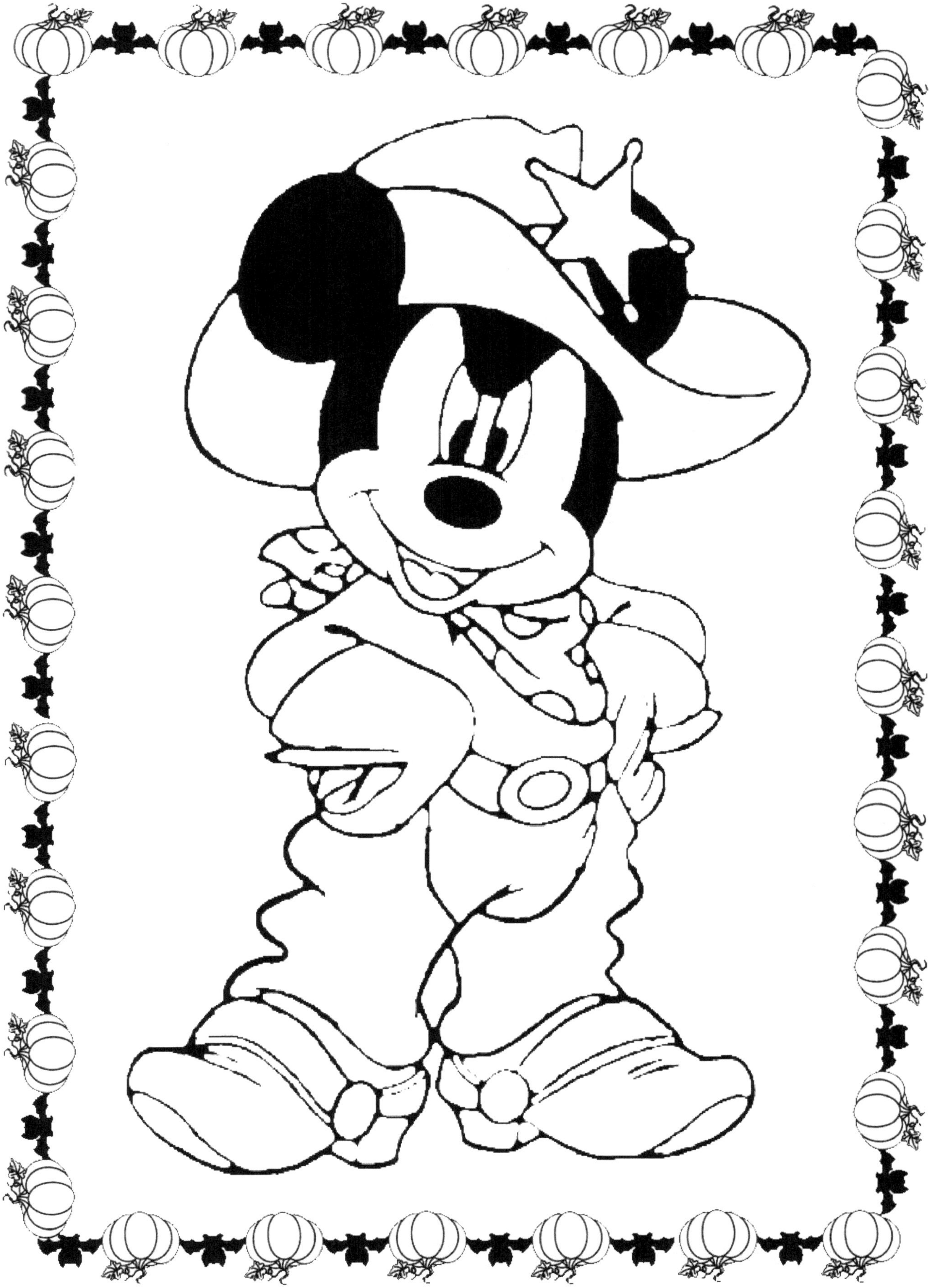

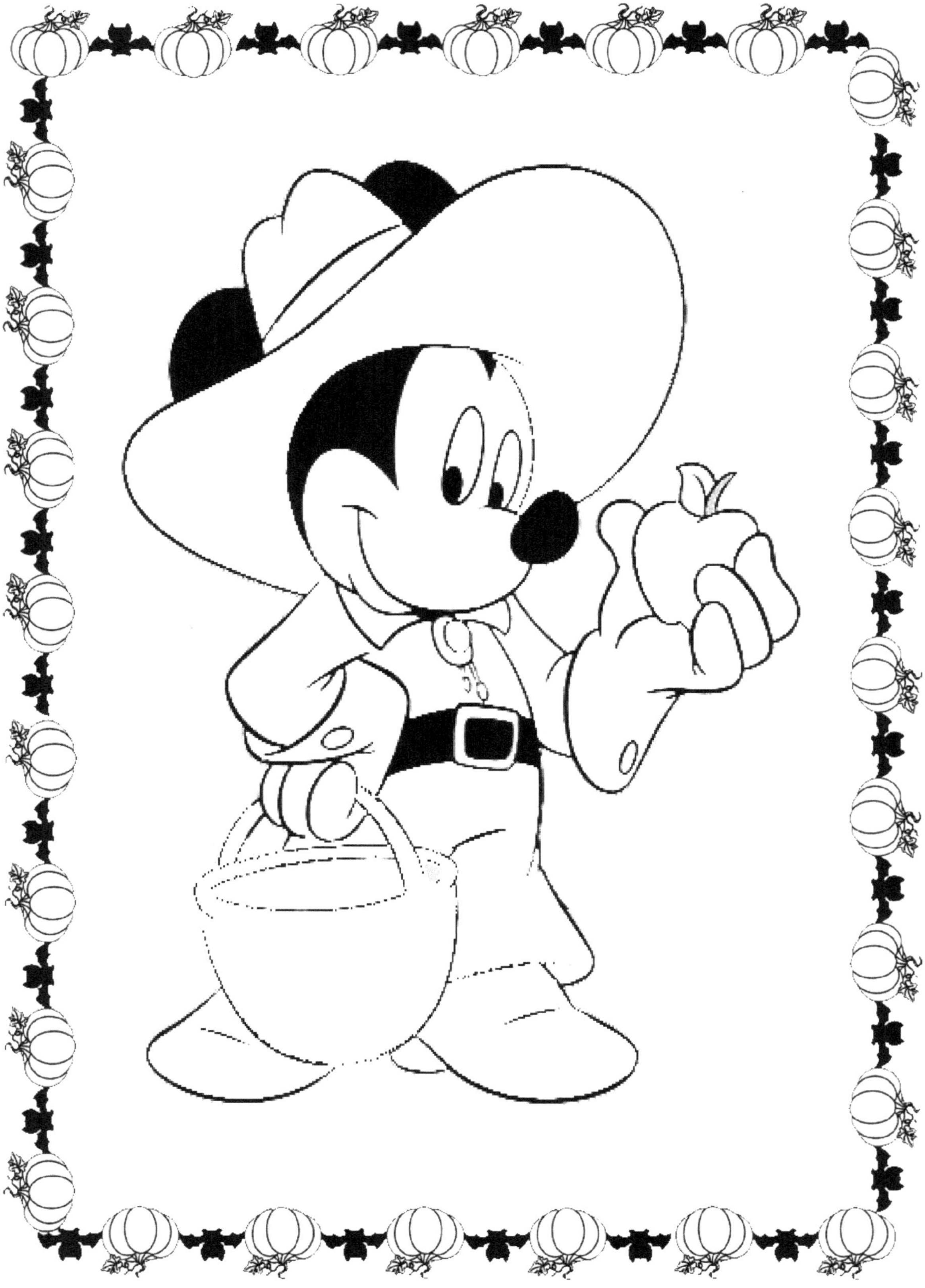

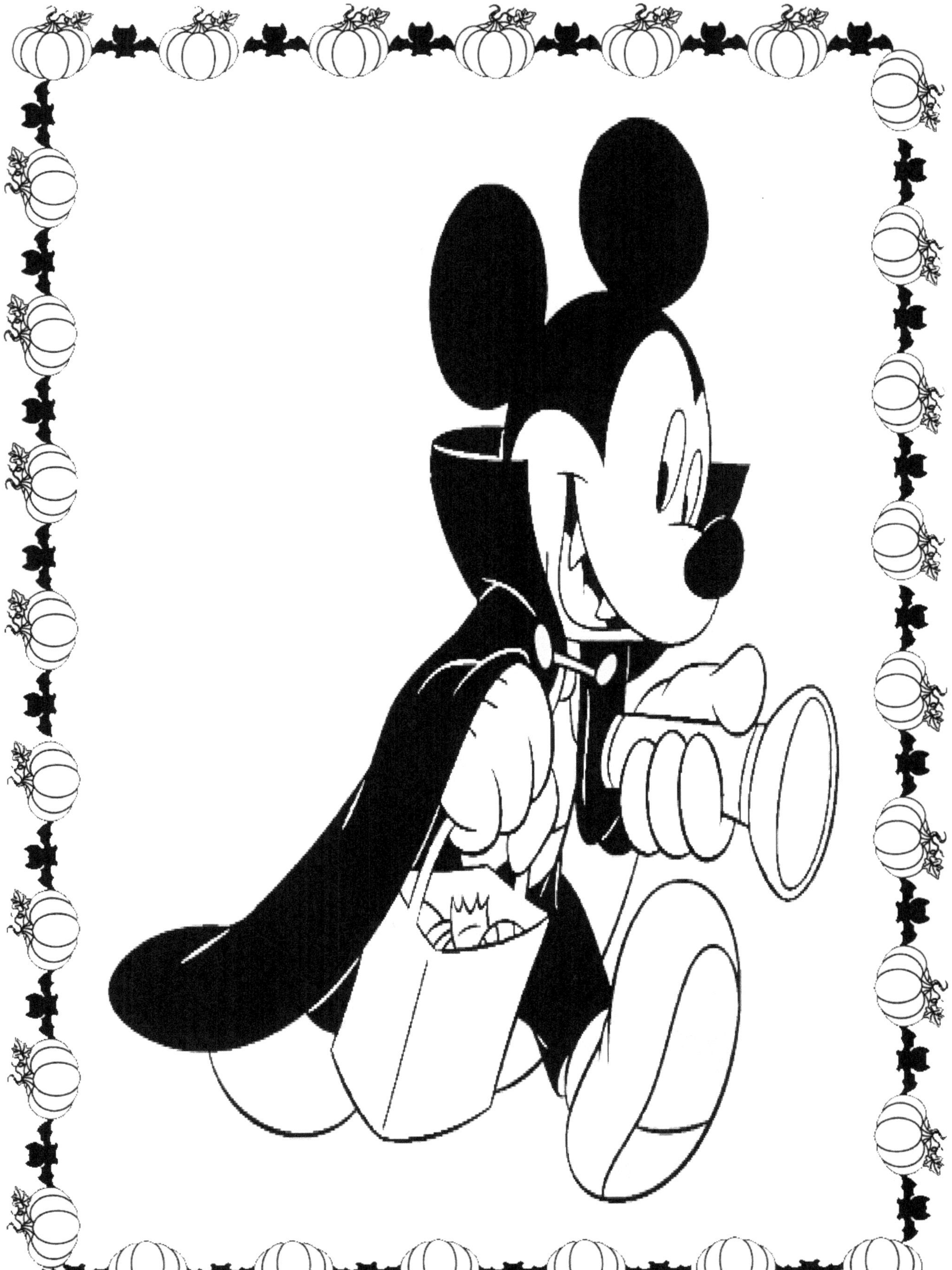

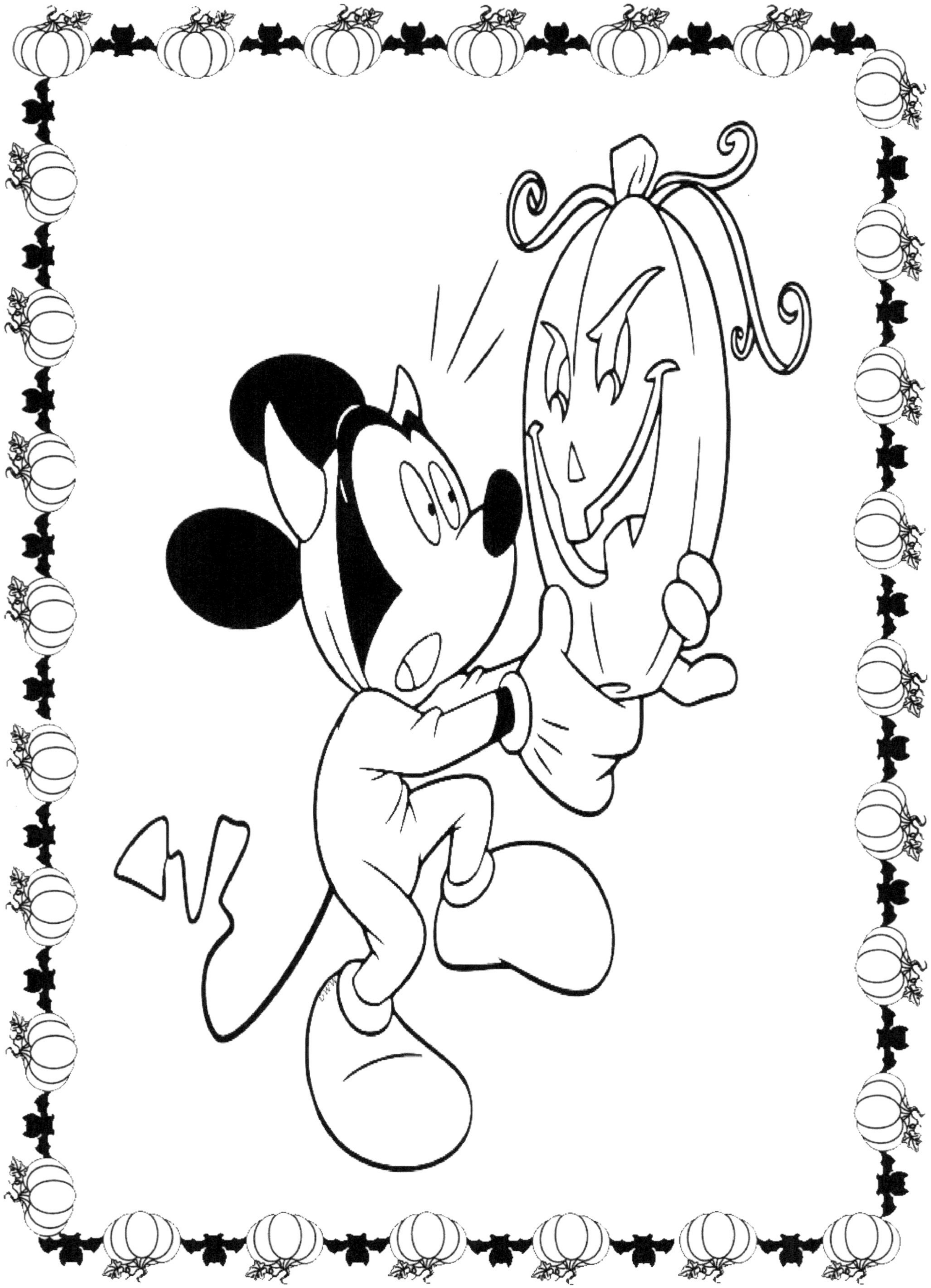

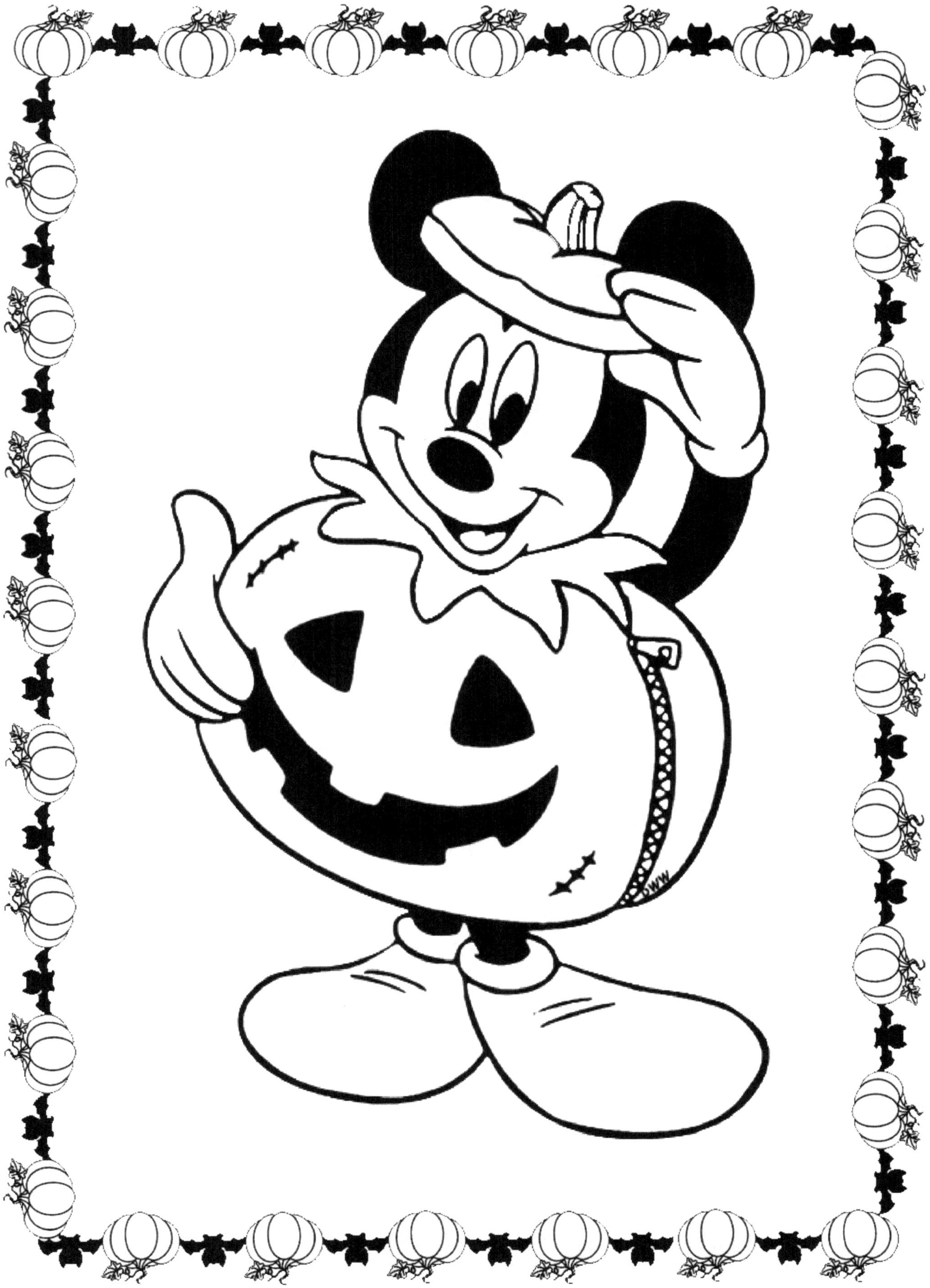

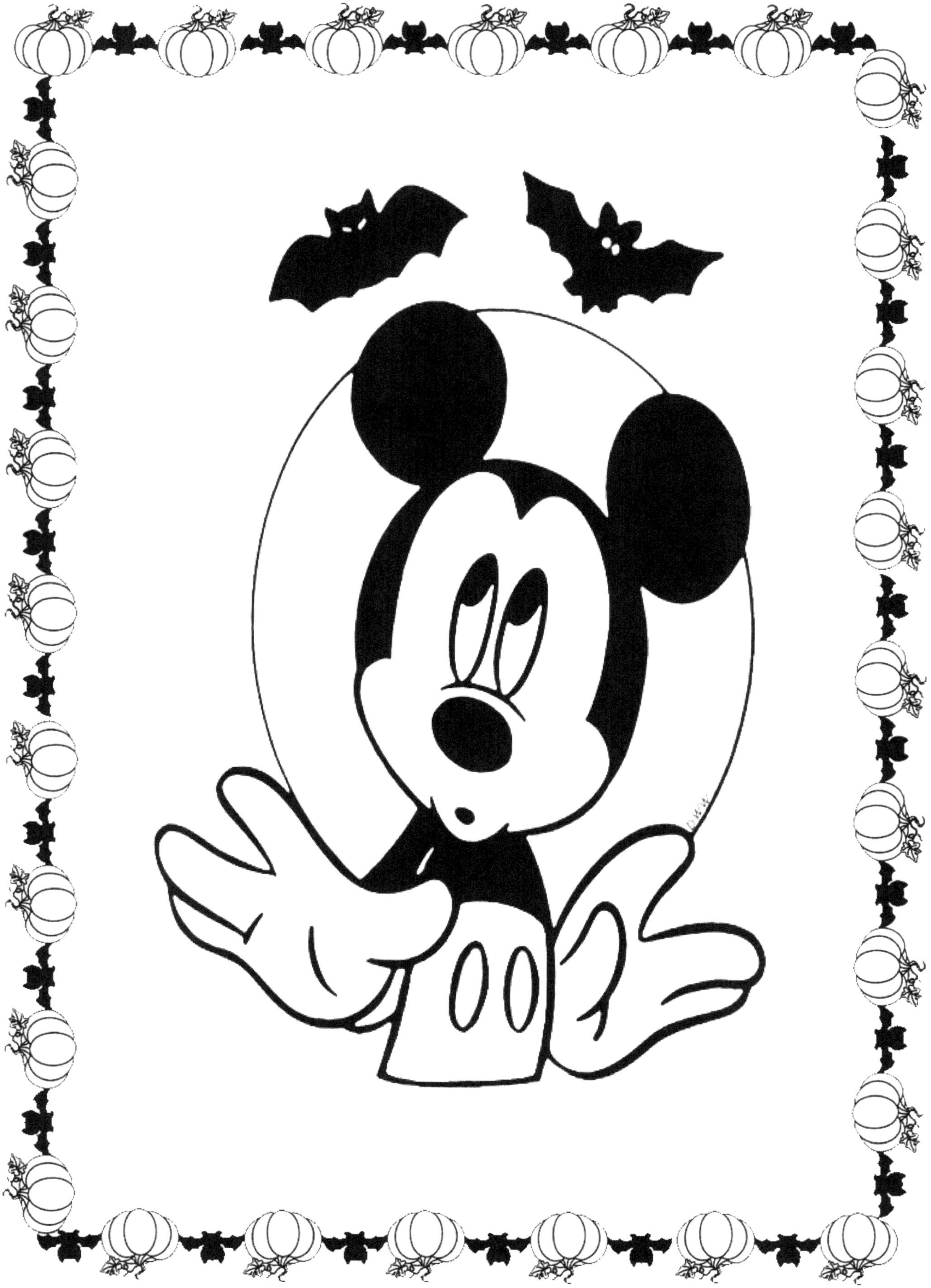

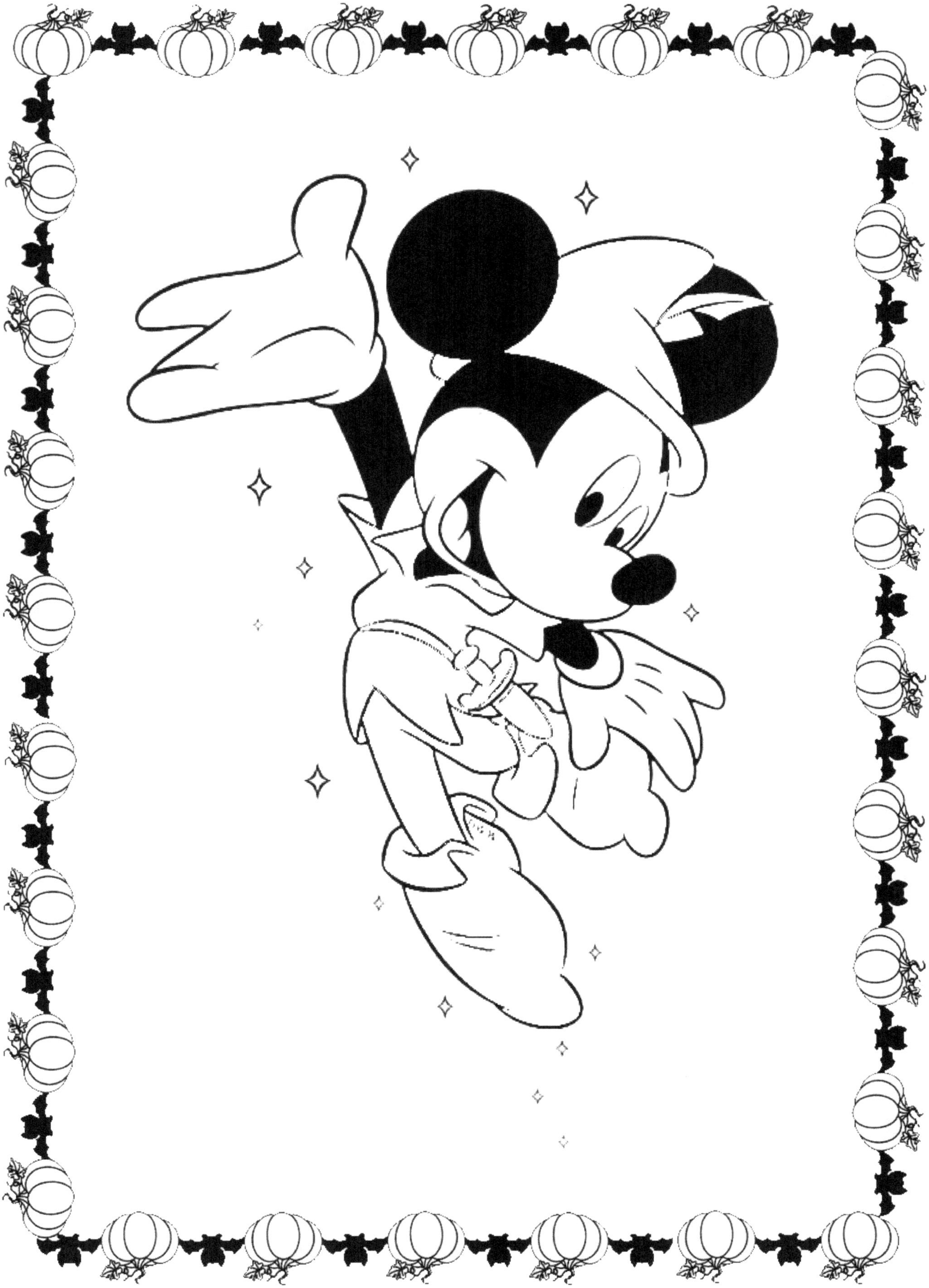

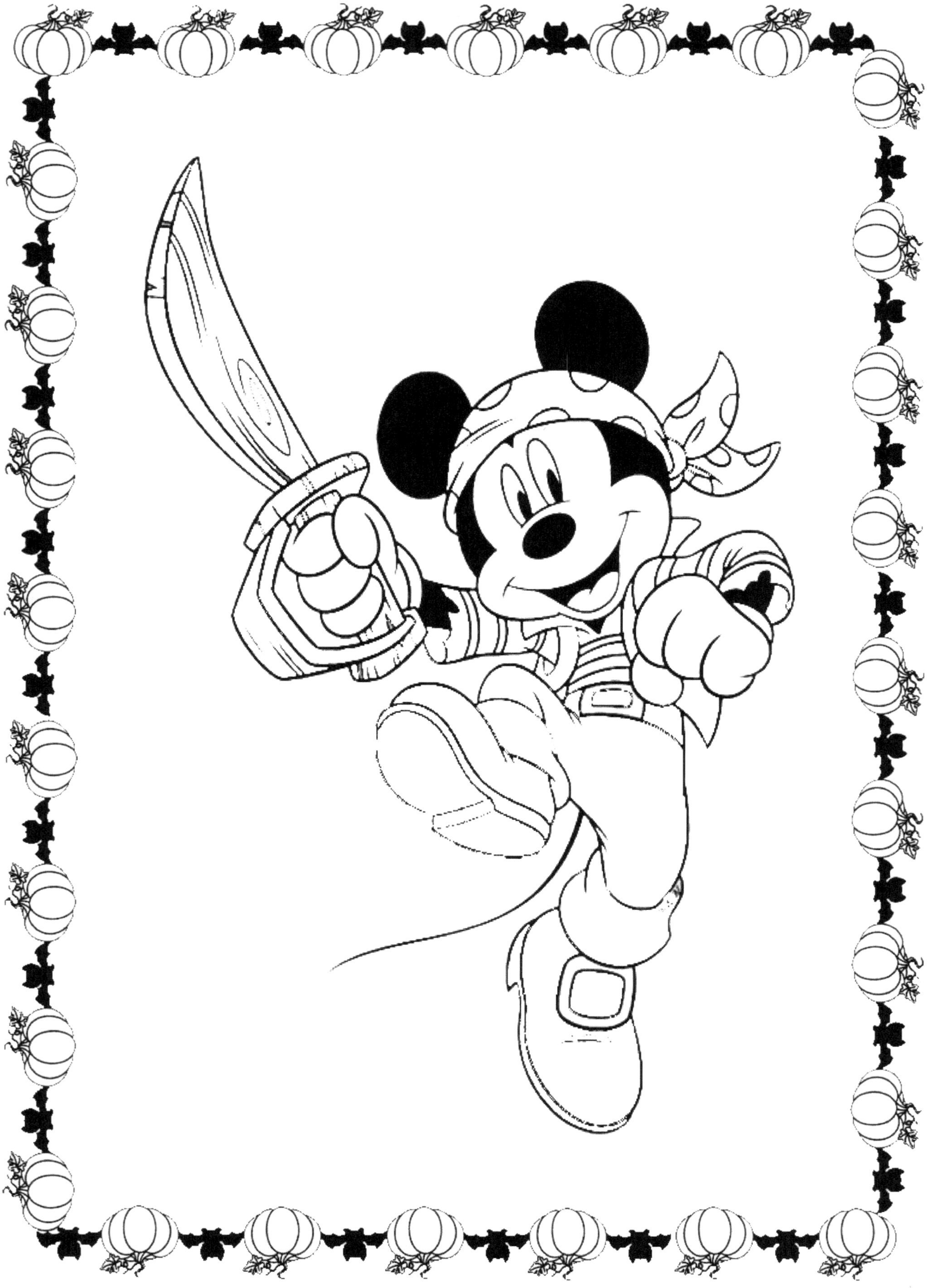

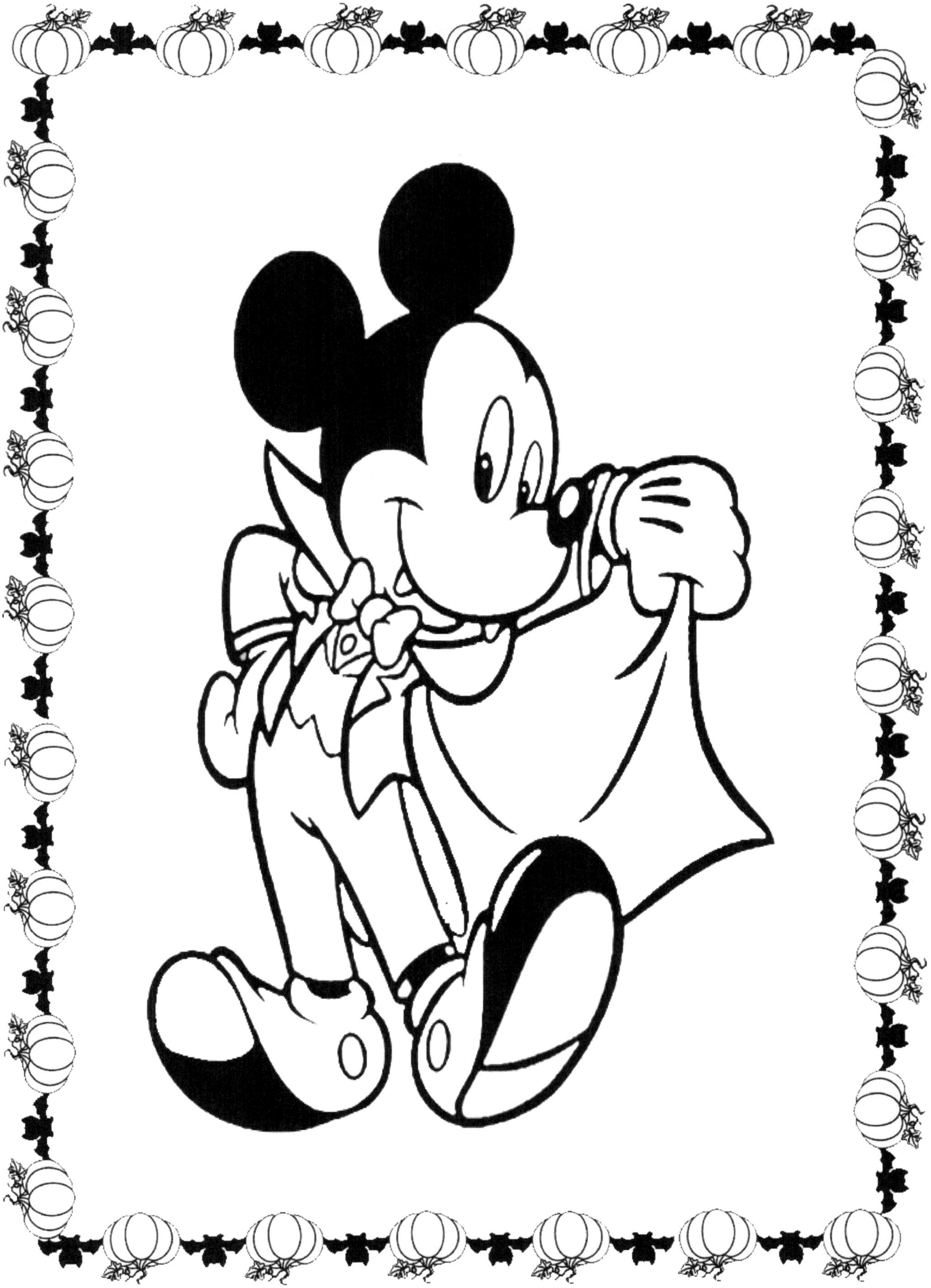

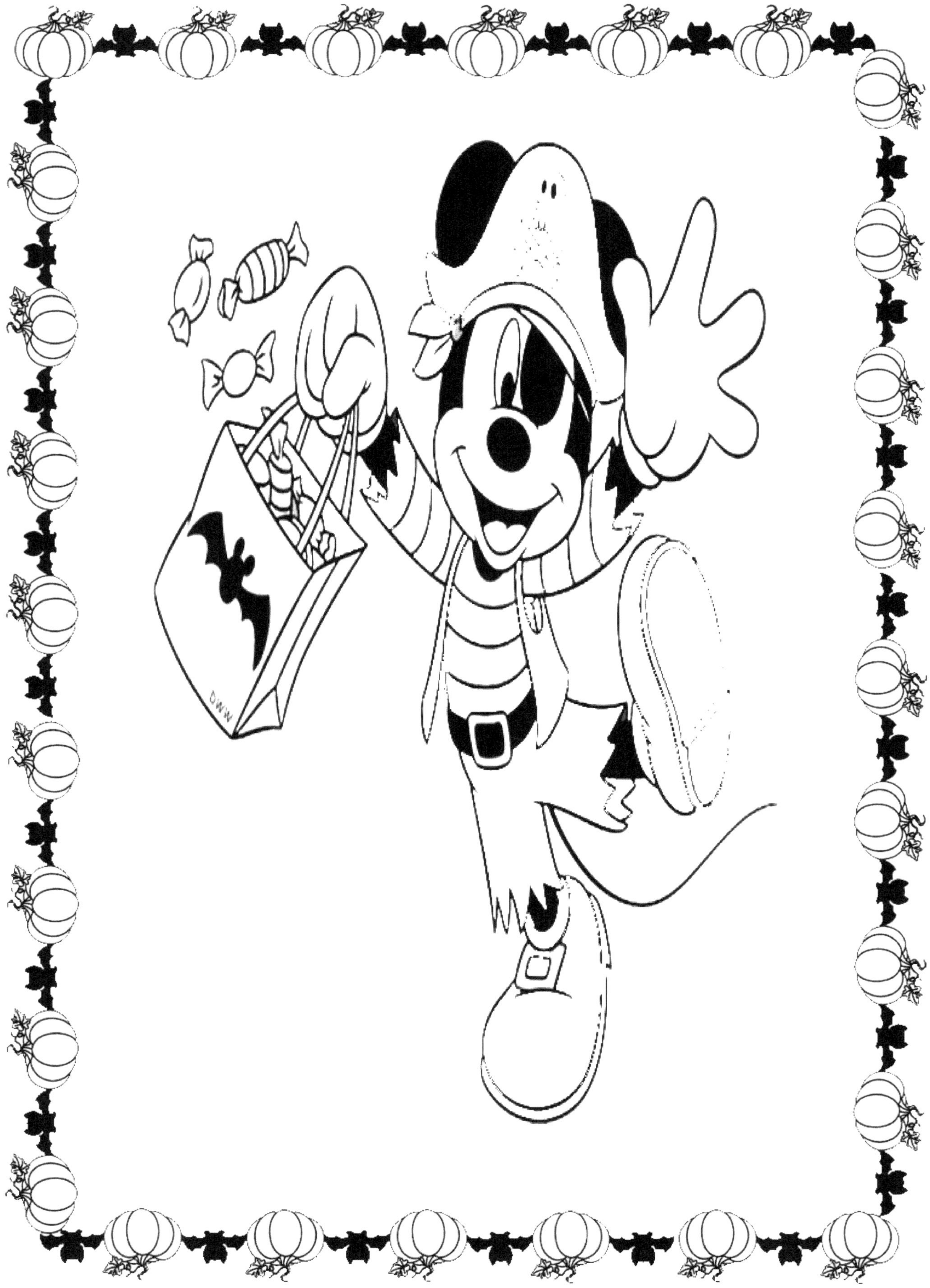

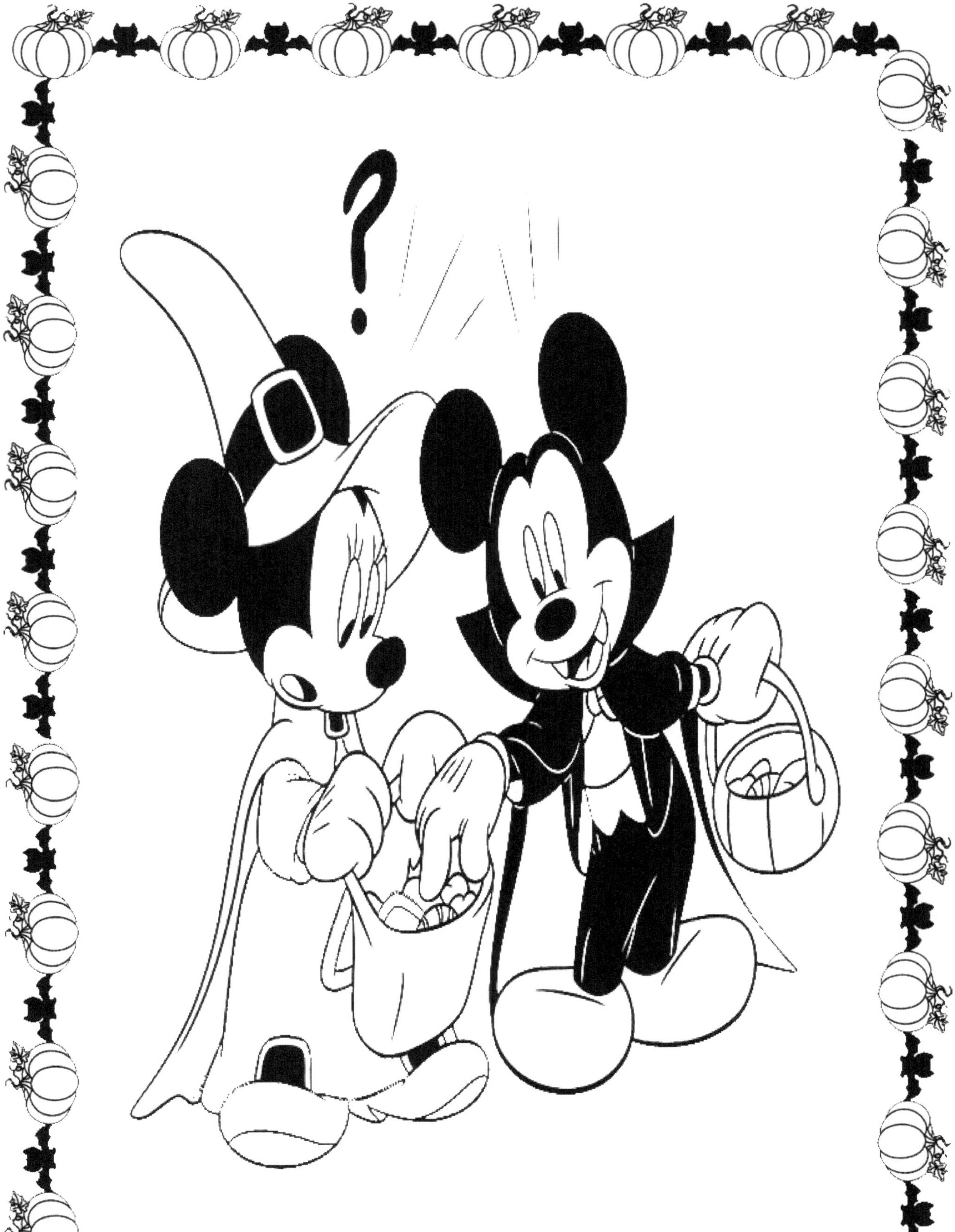

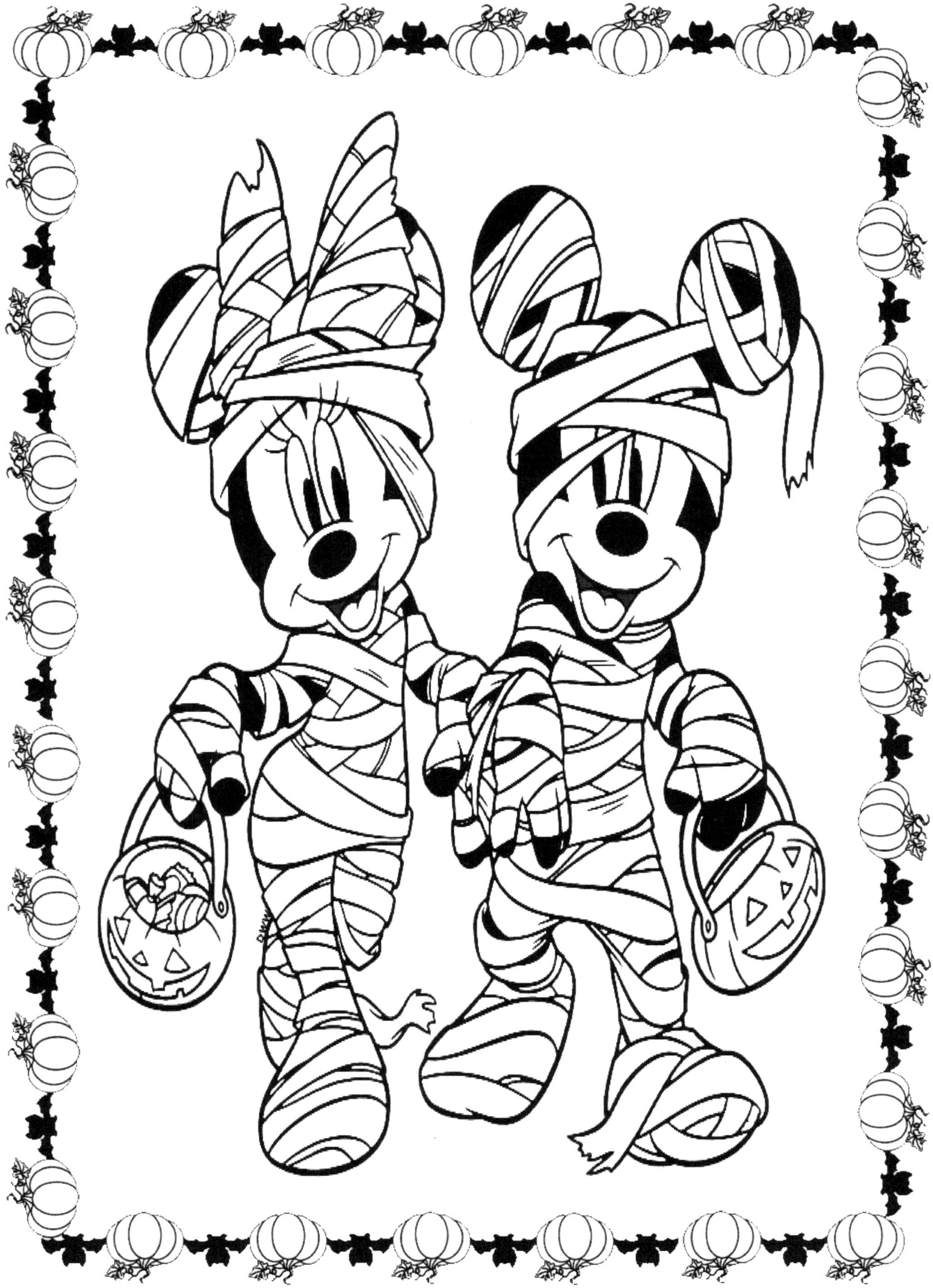

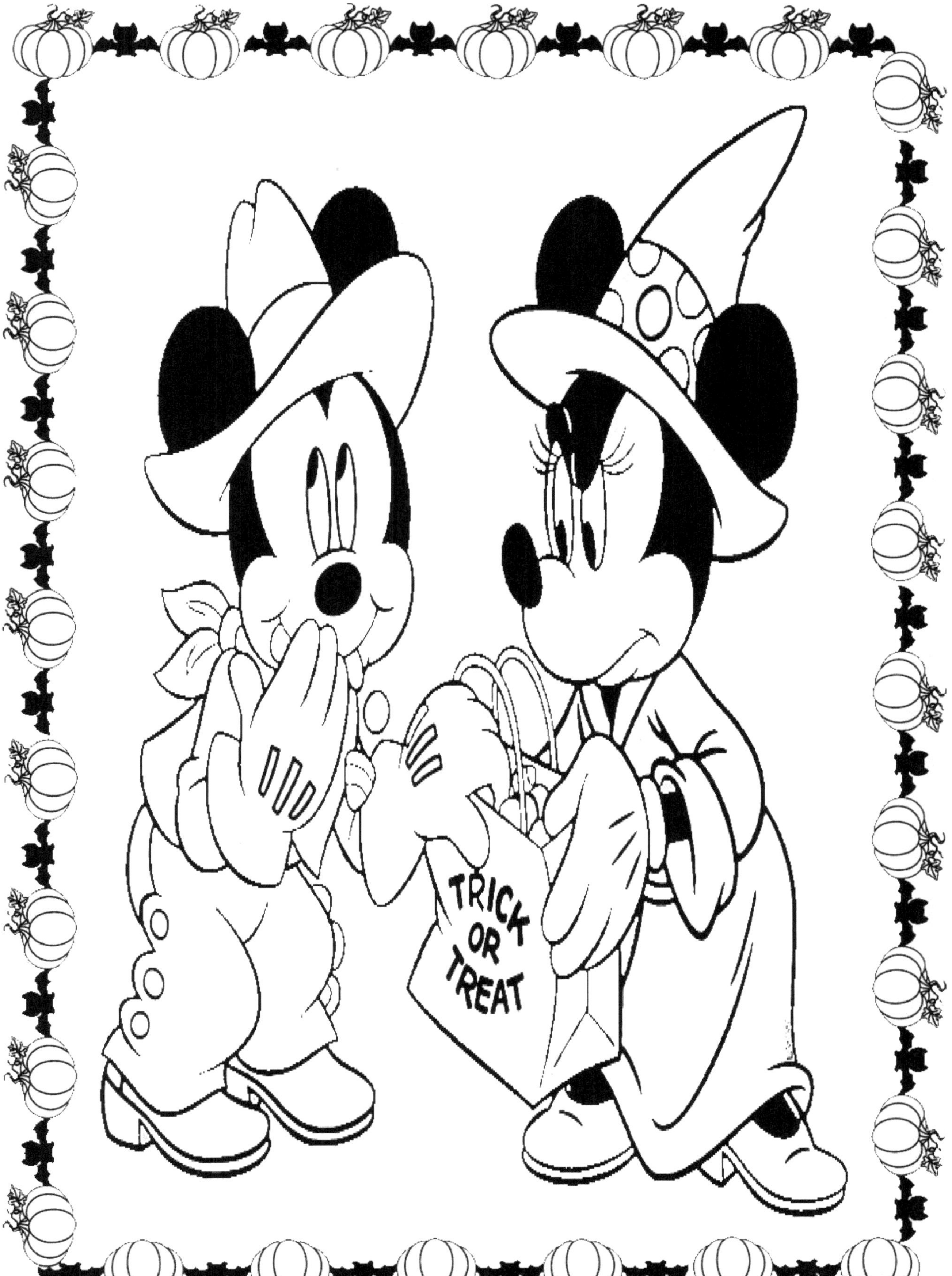
TRICK
OR
TREAT

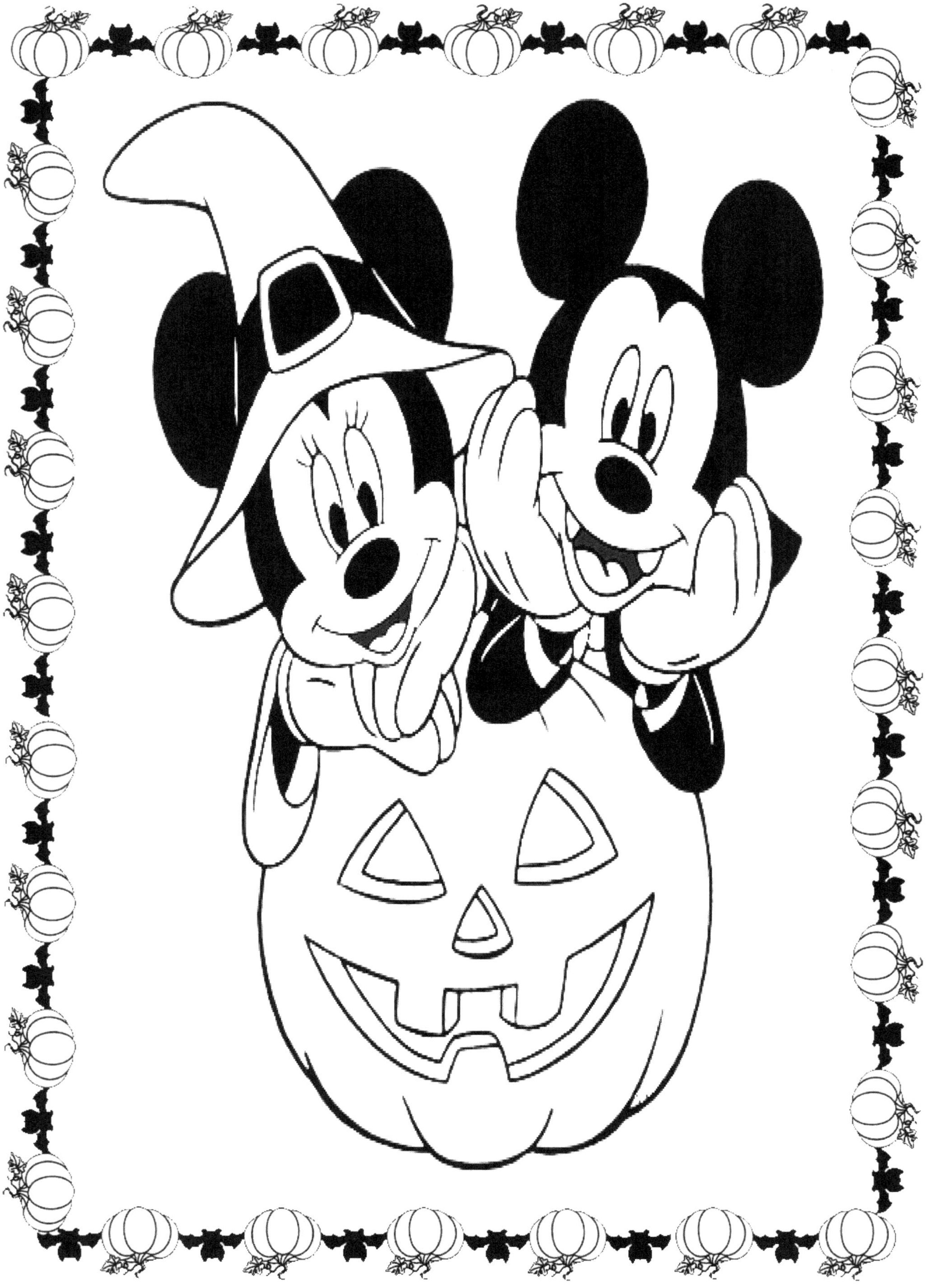

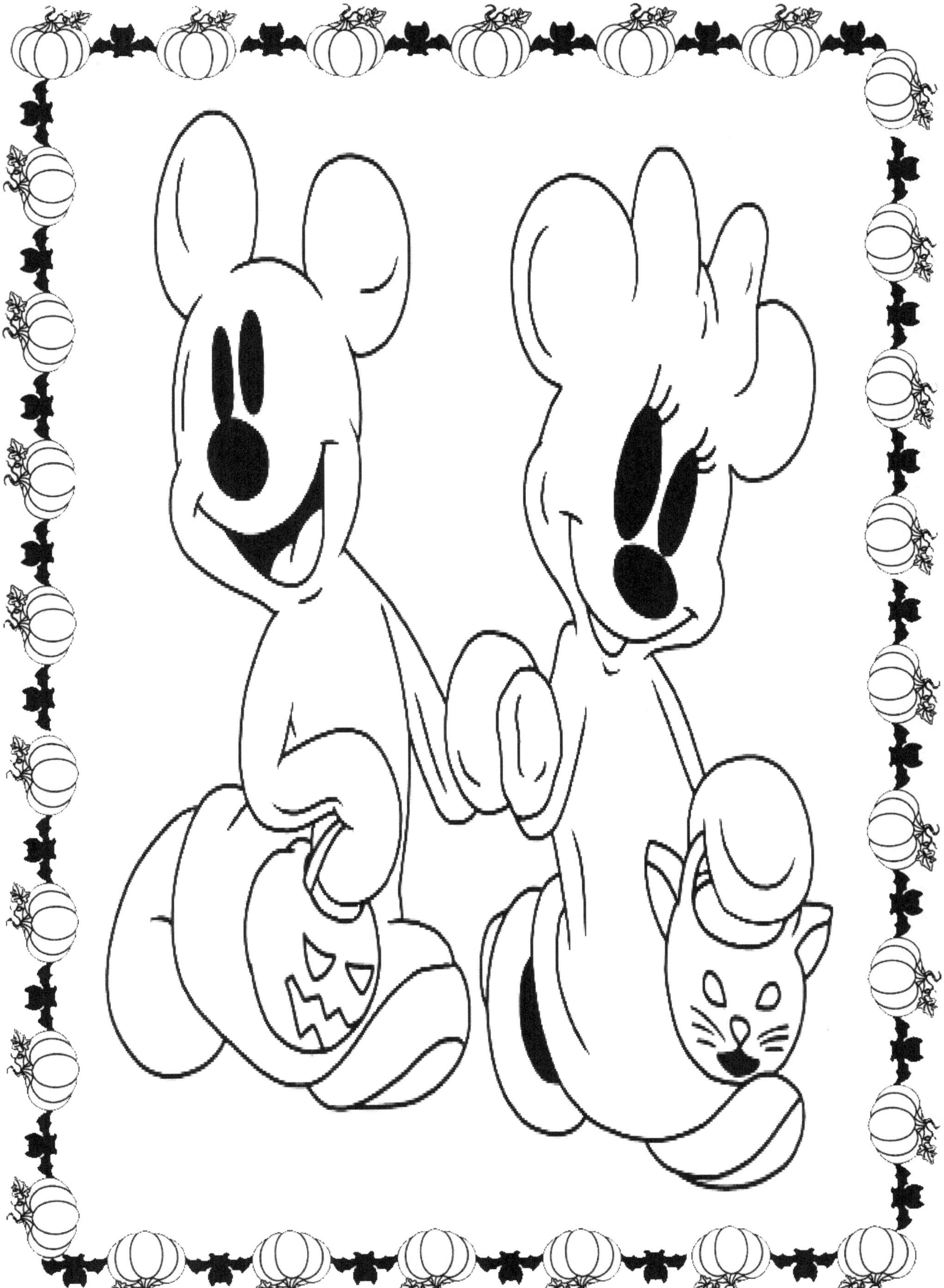

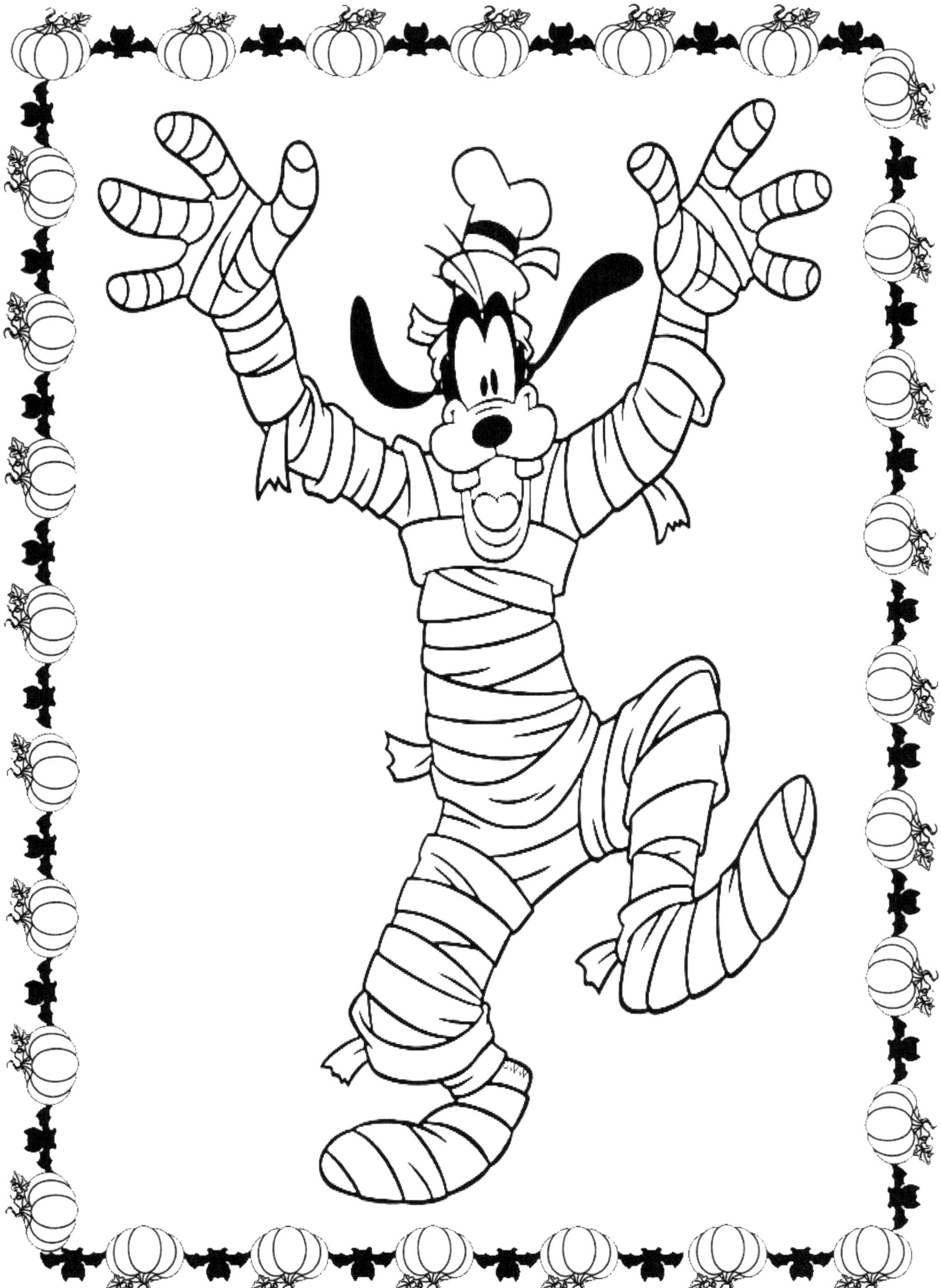

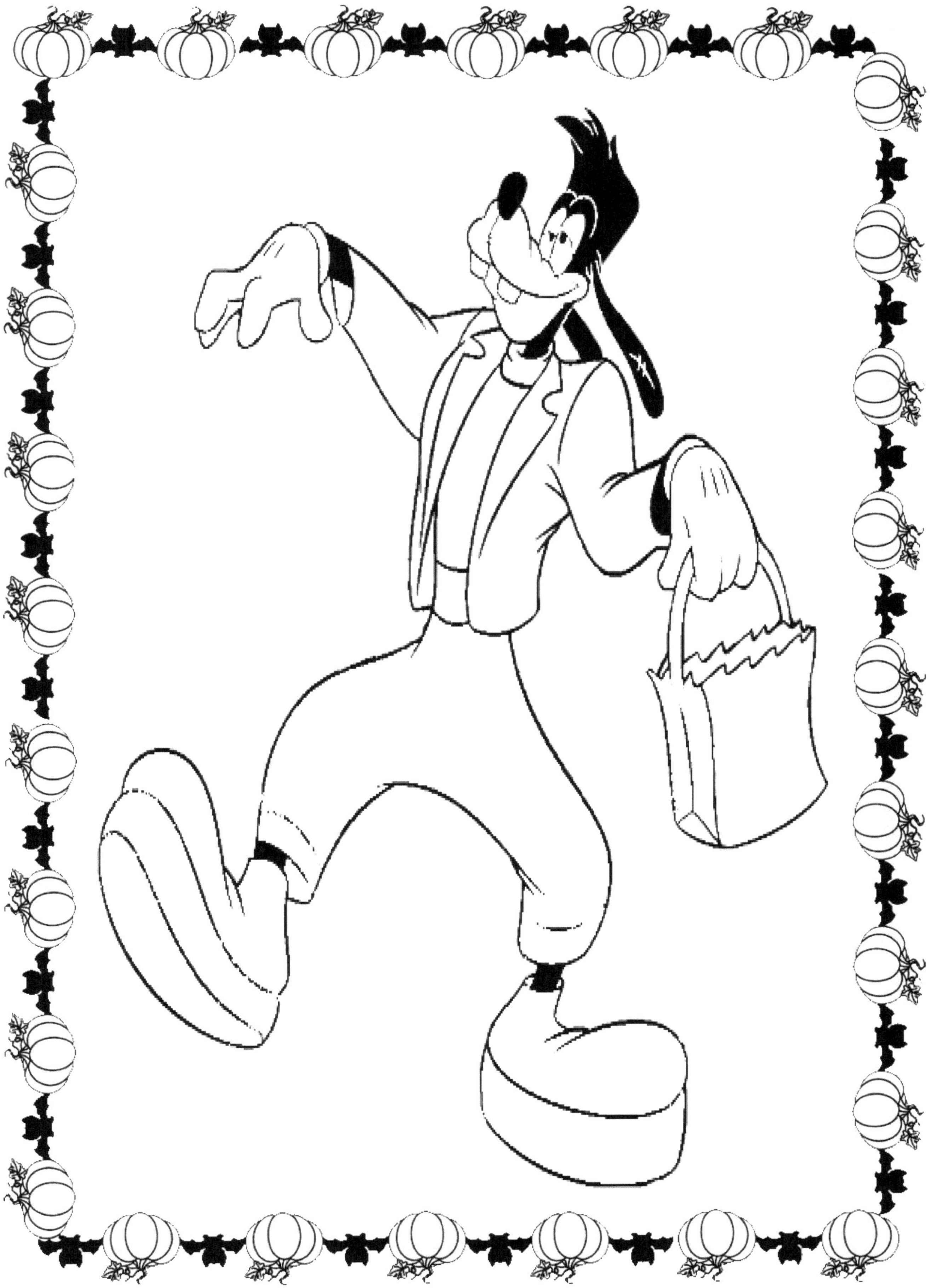

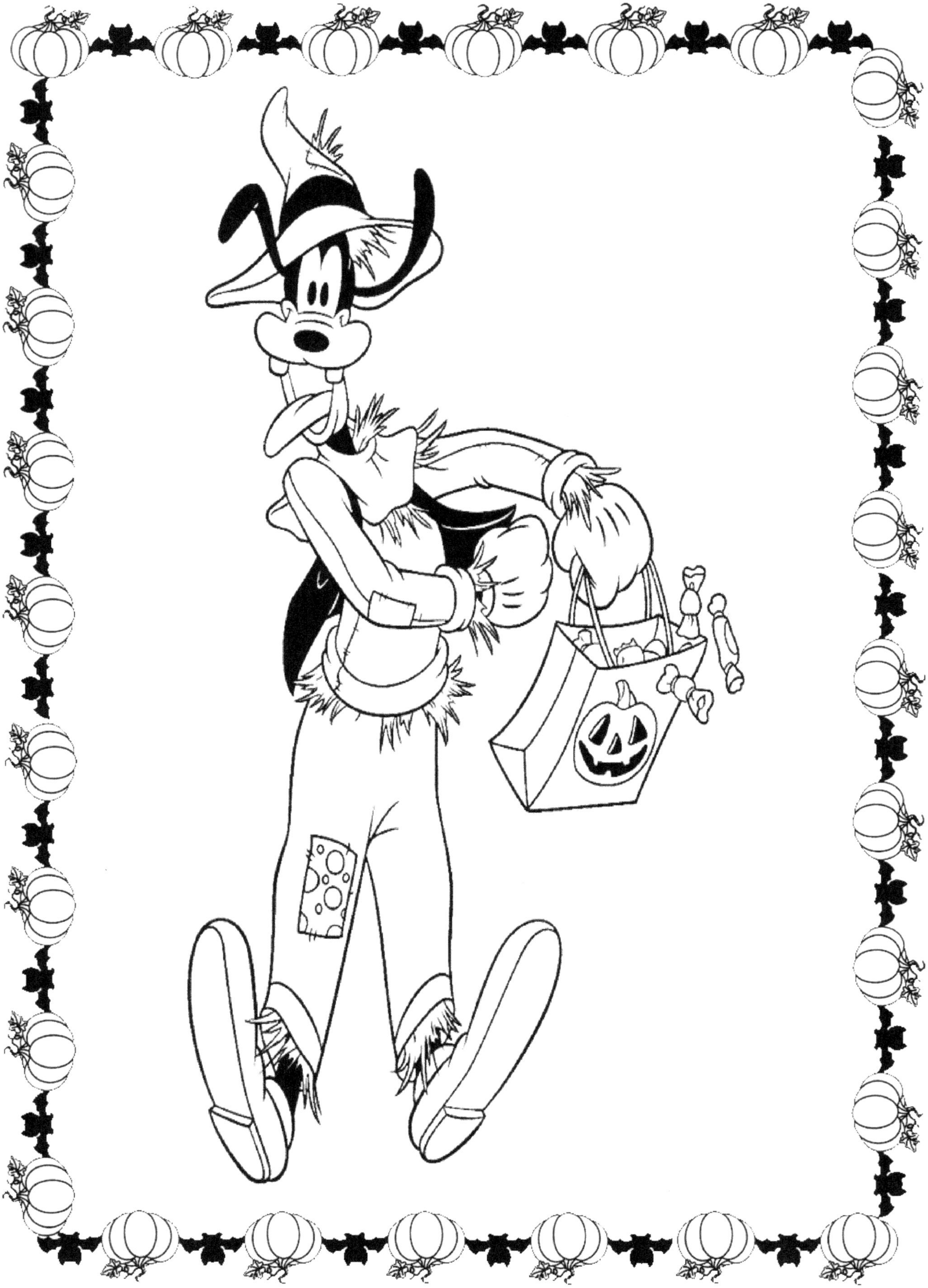

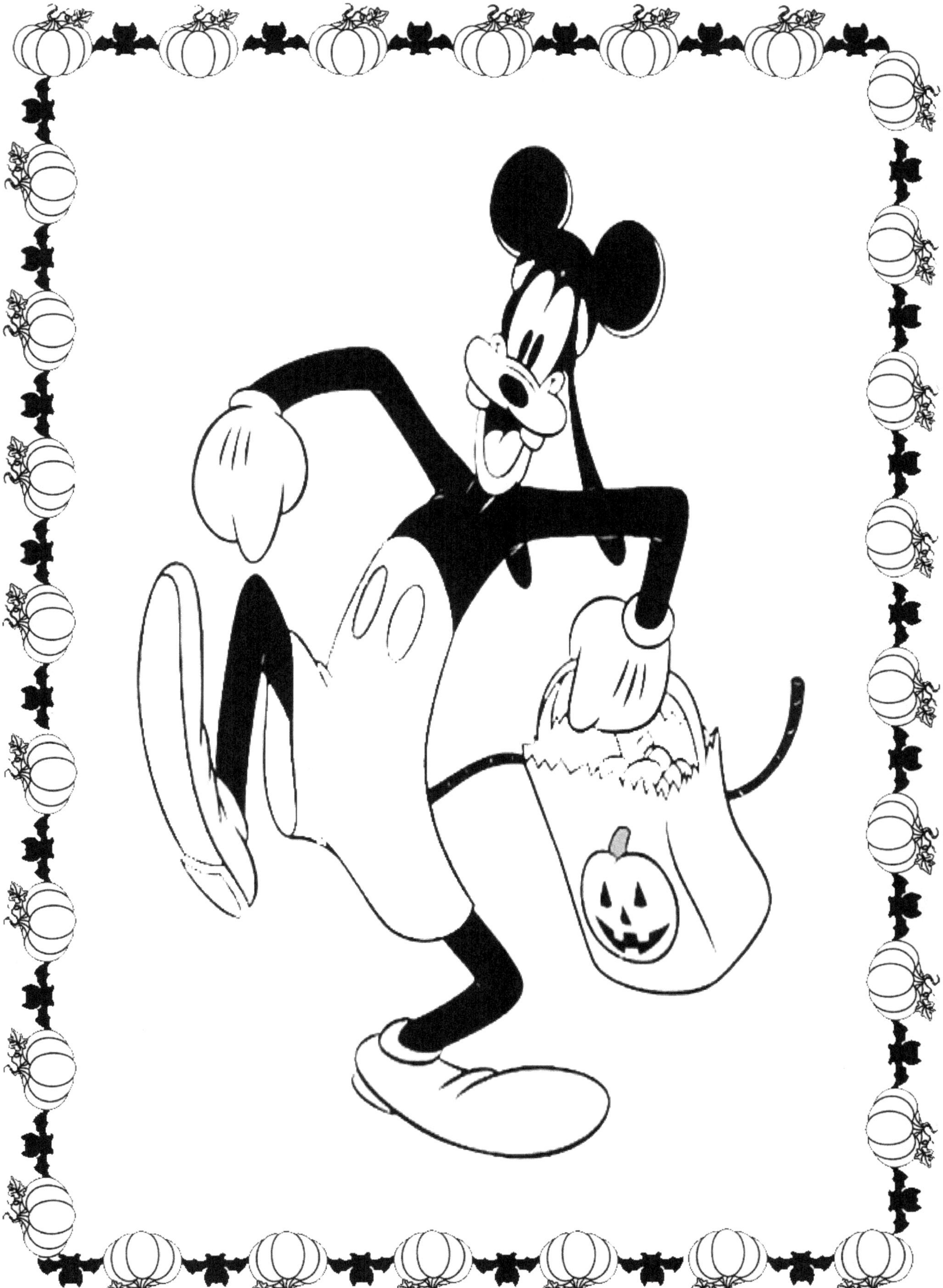

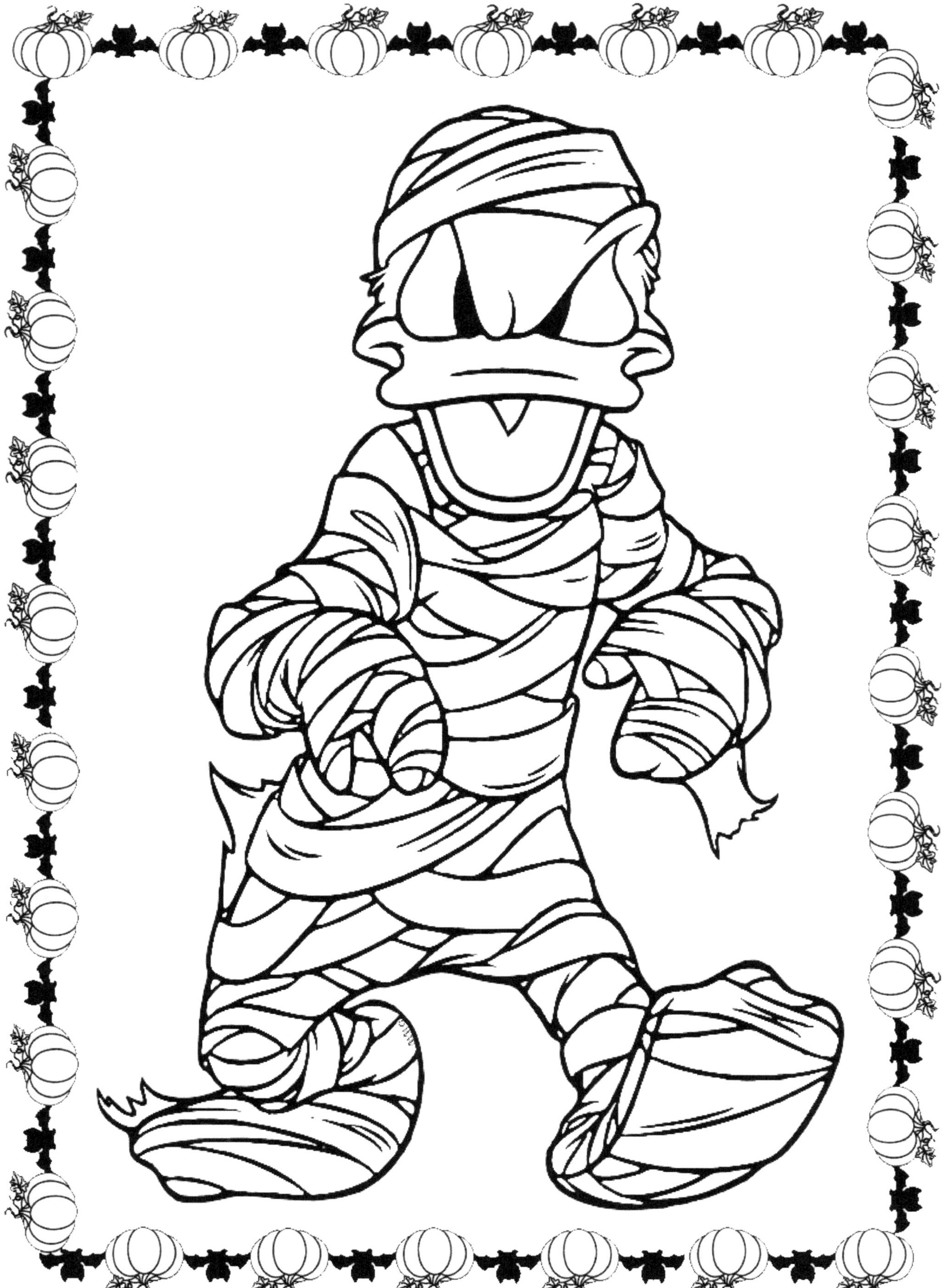

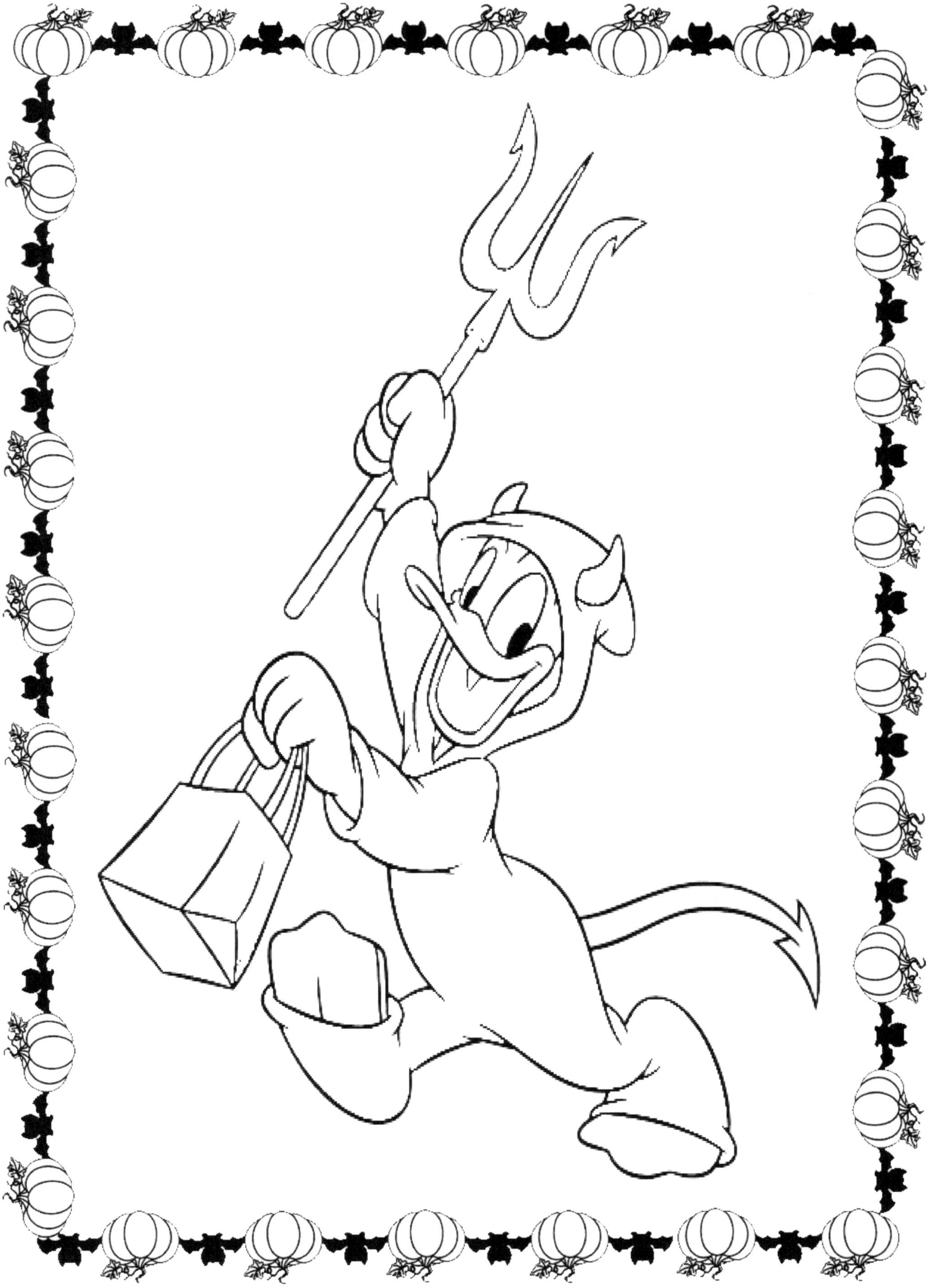

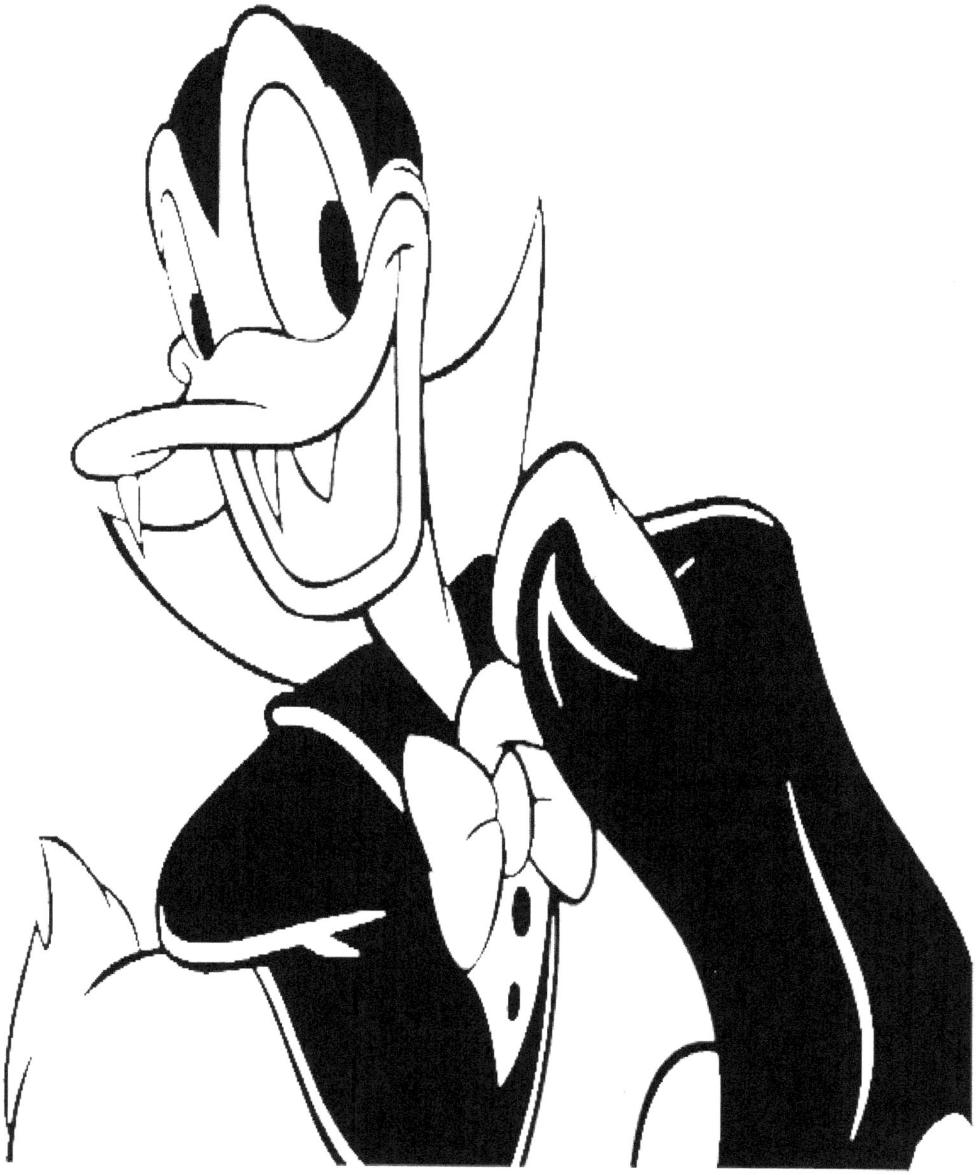

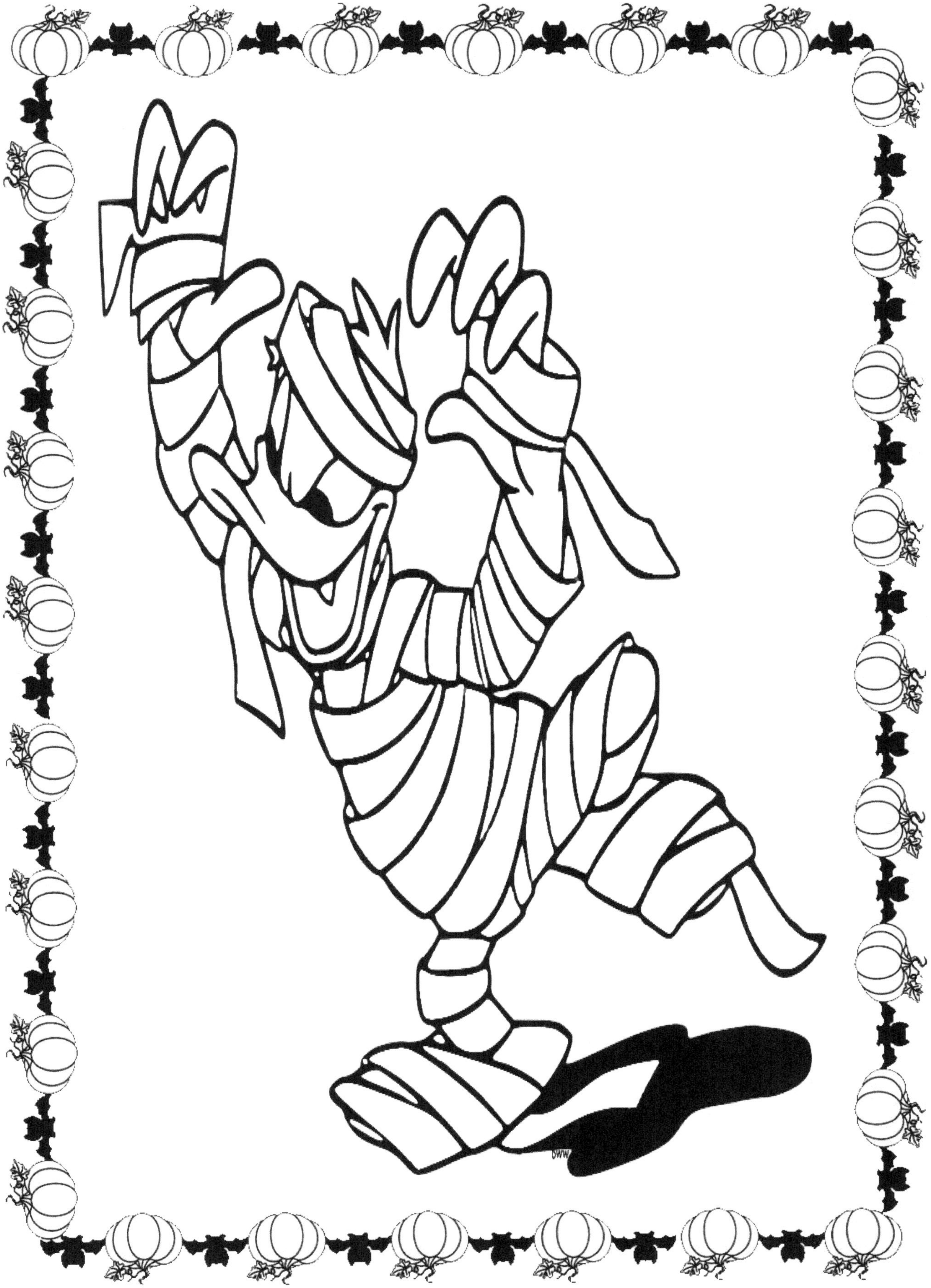

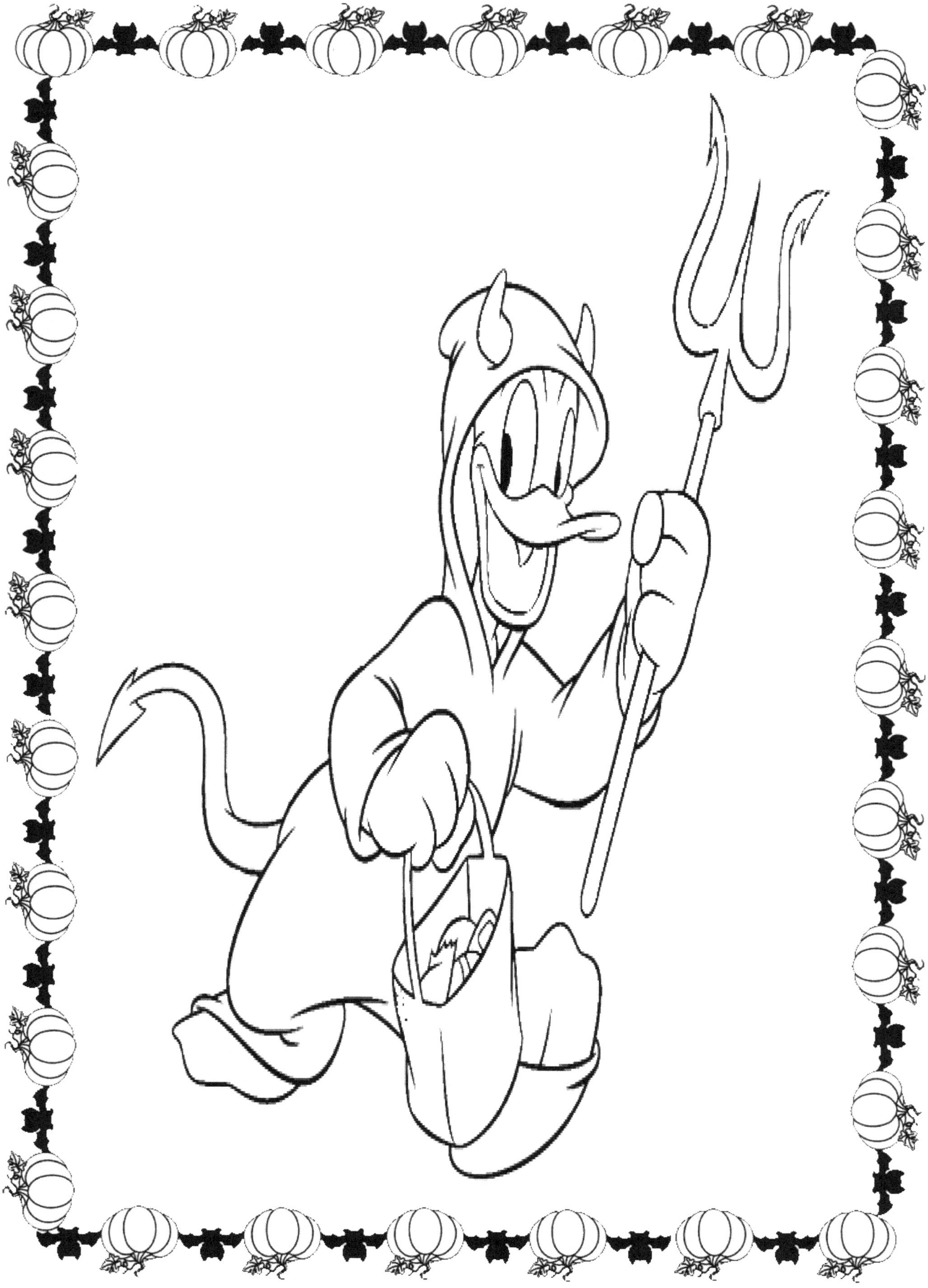

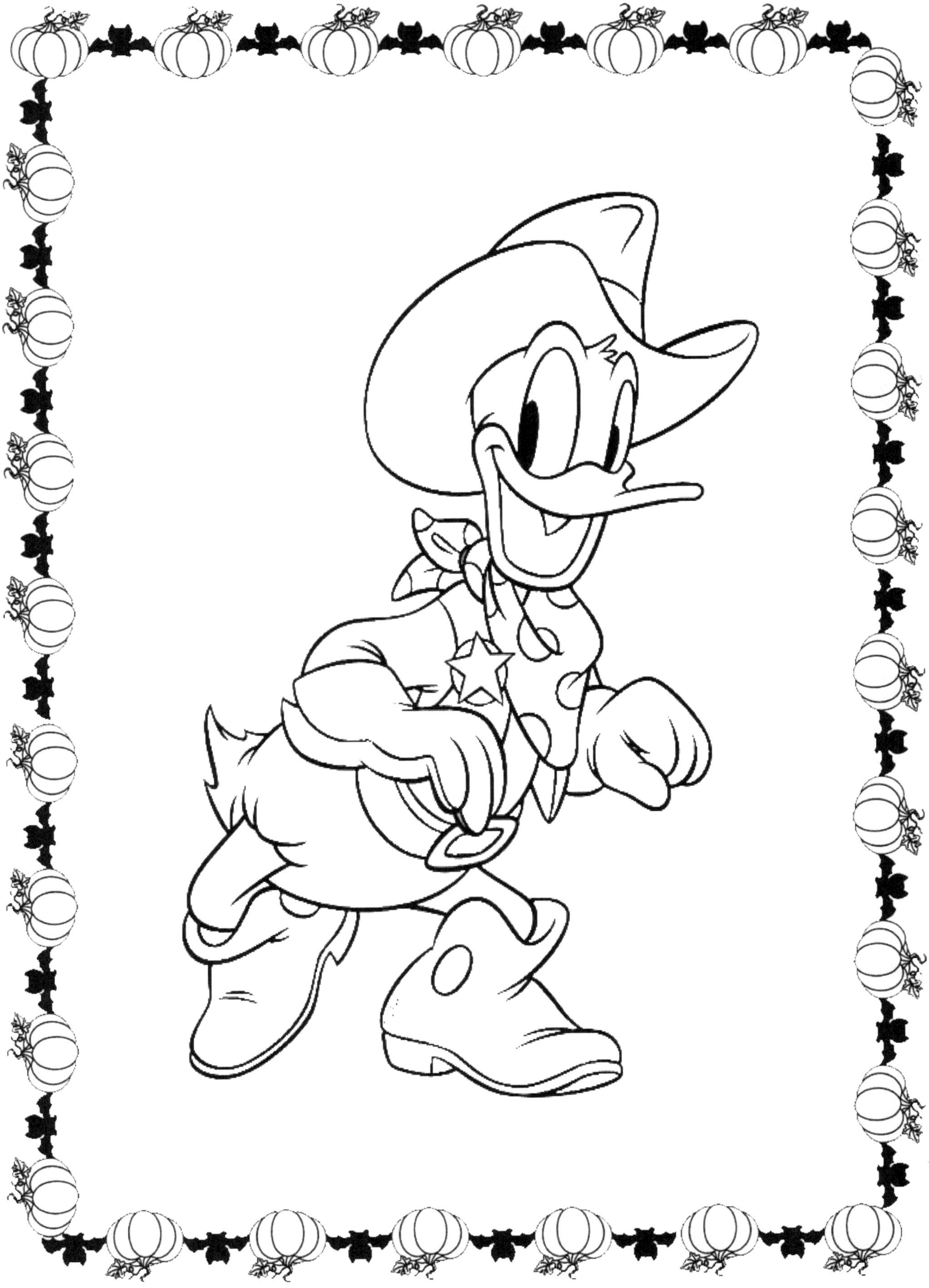

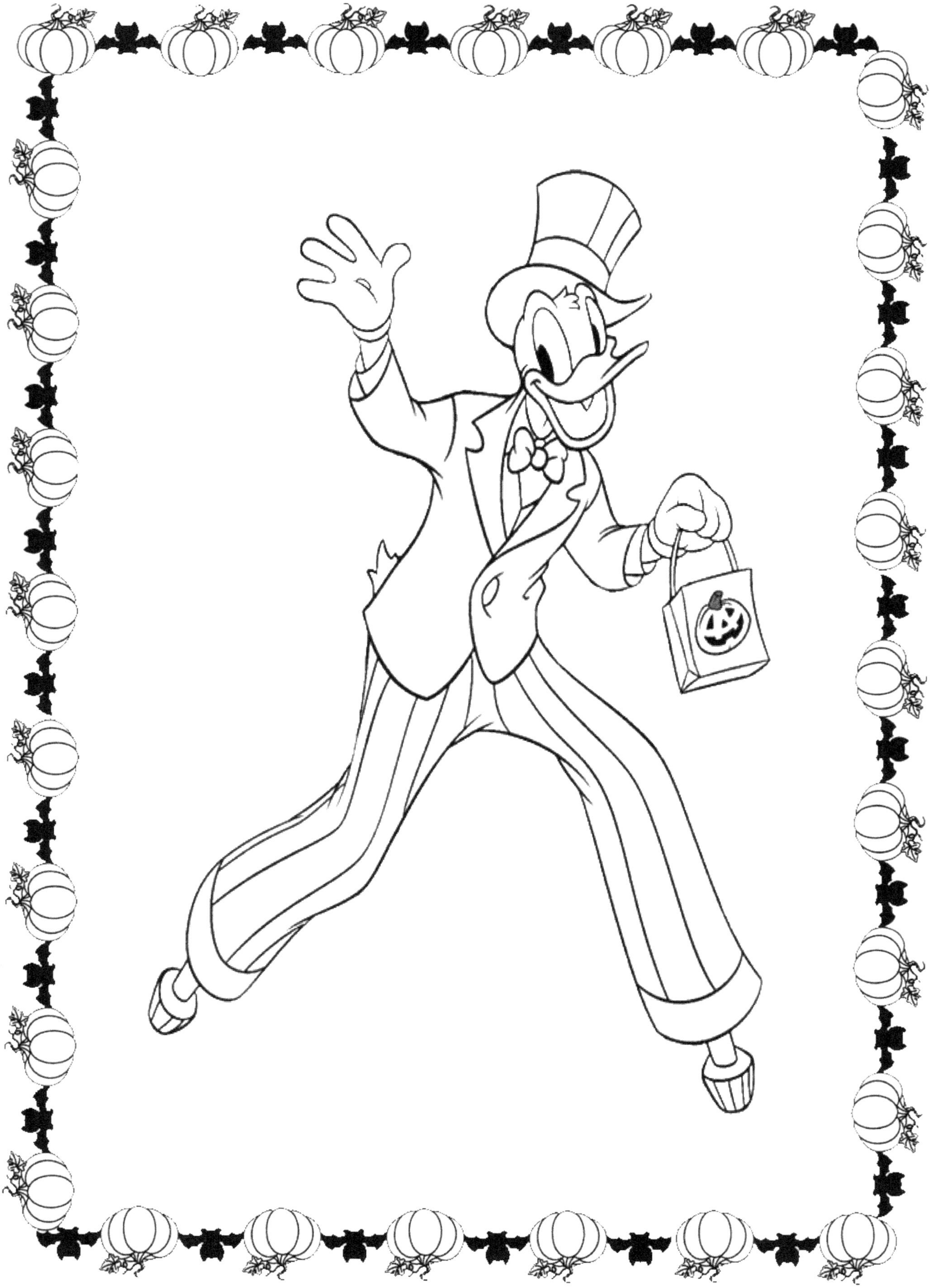

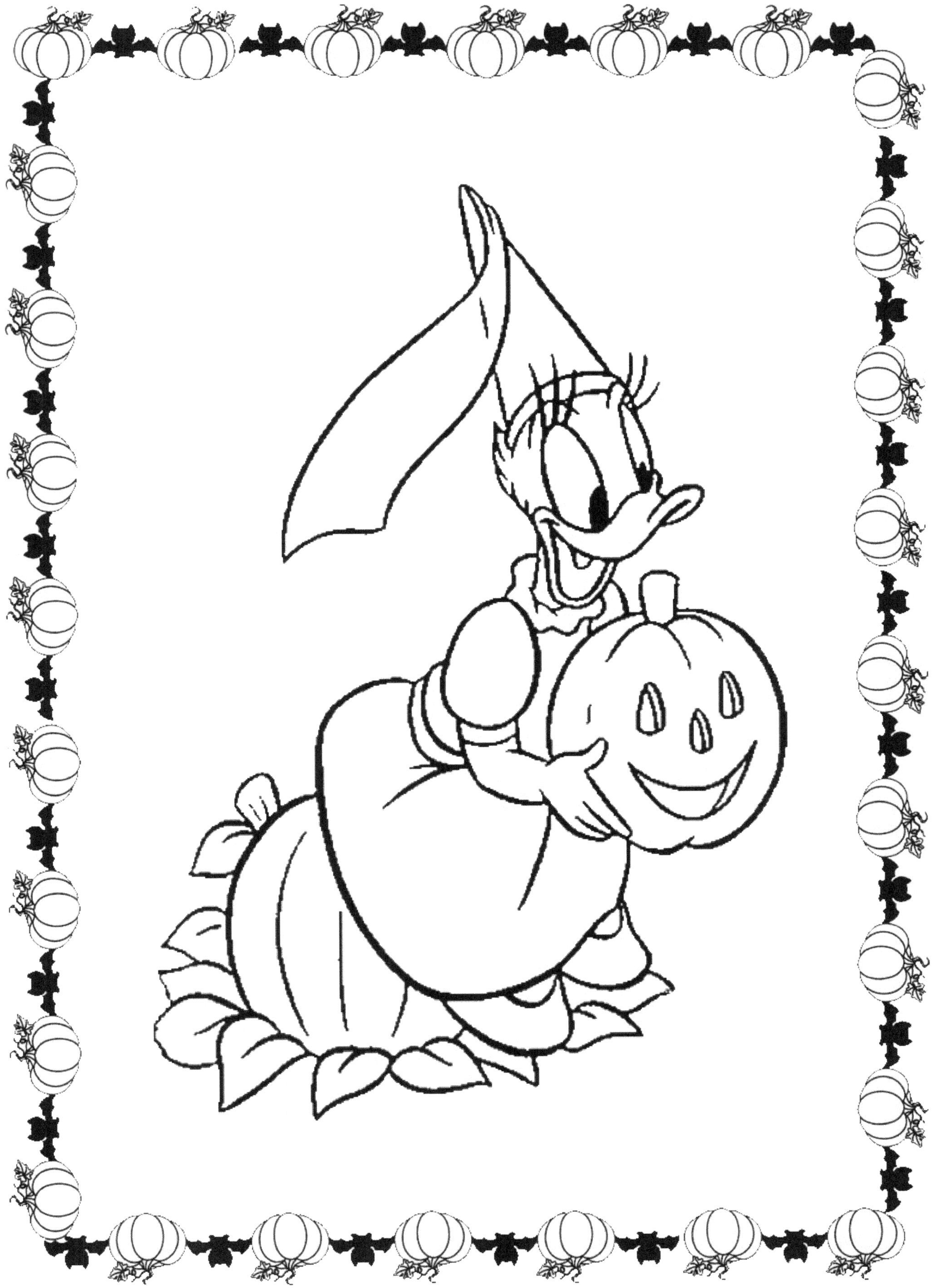

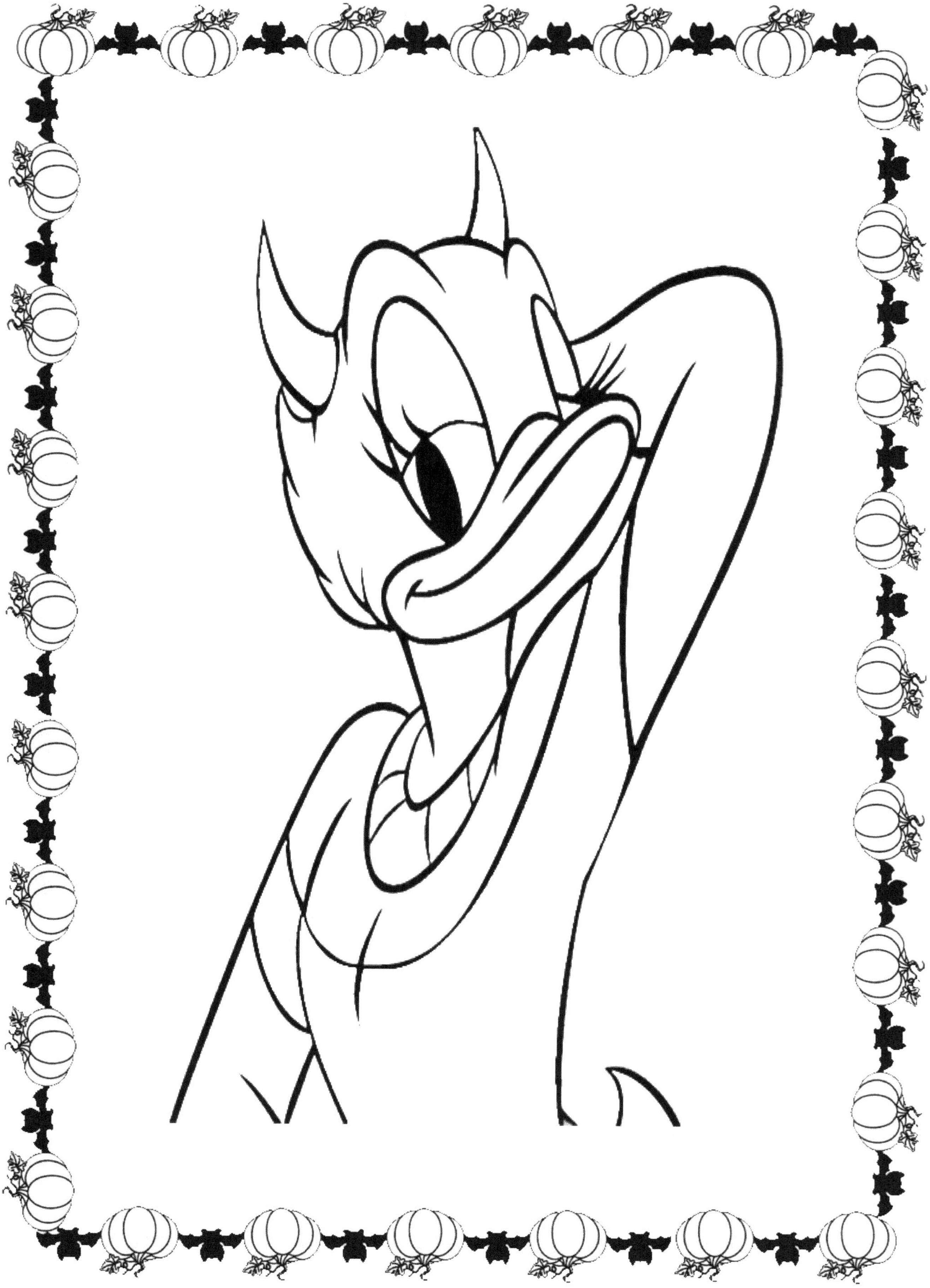

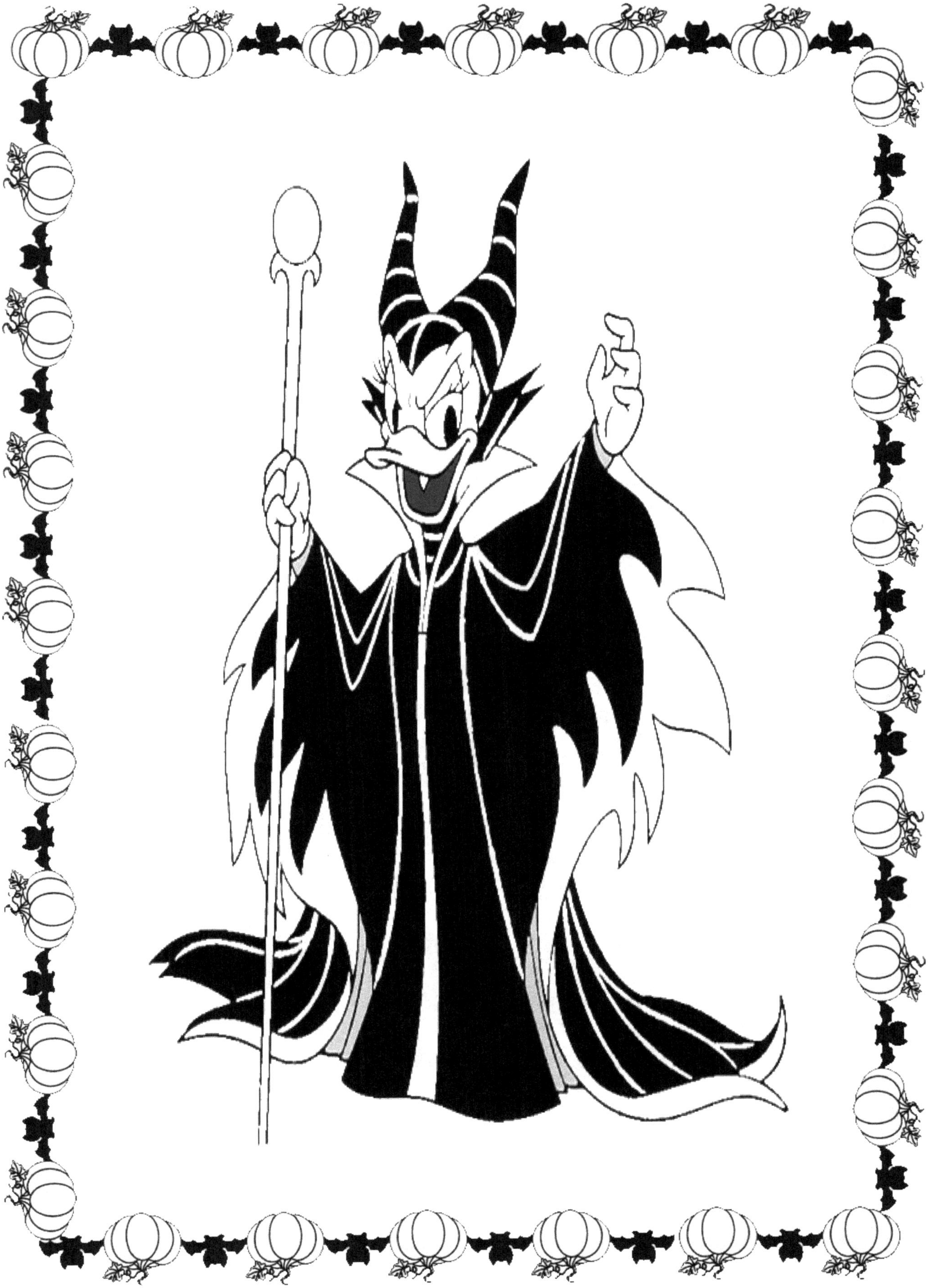

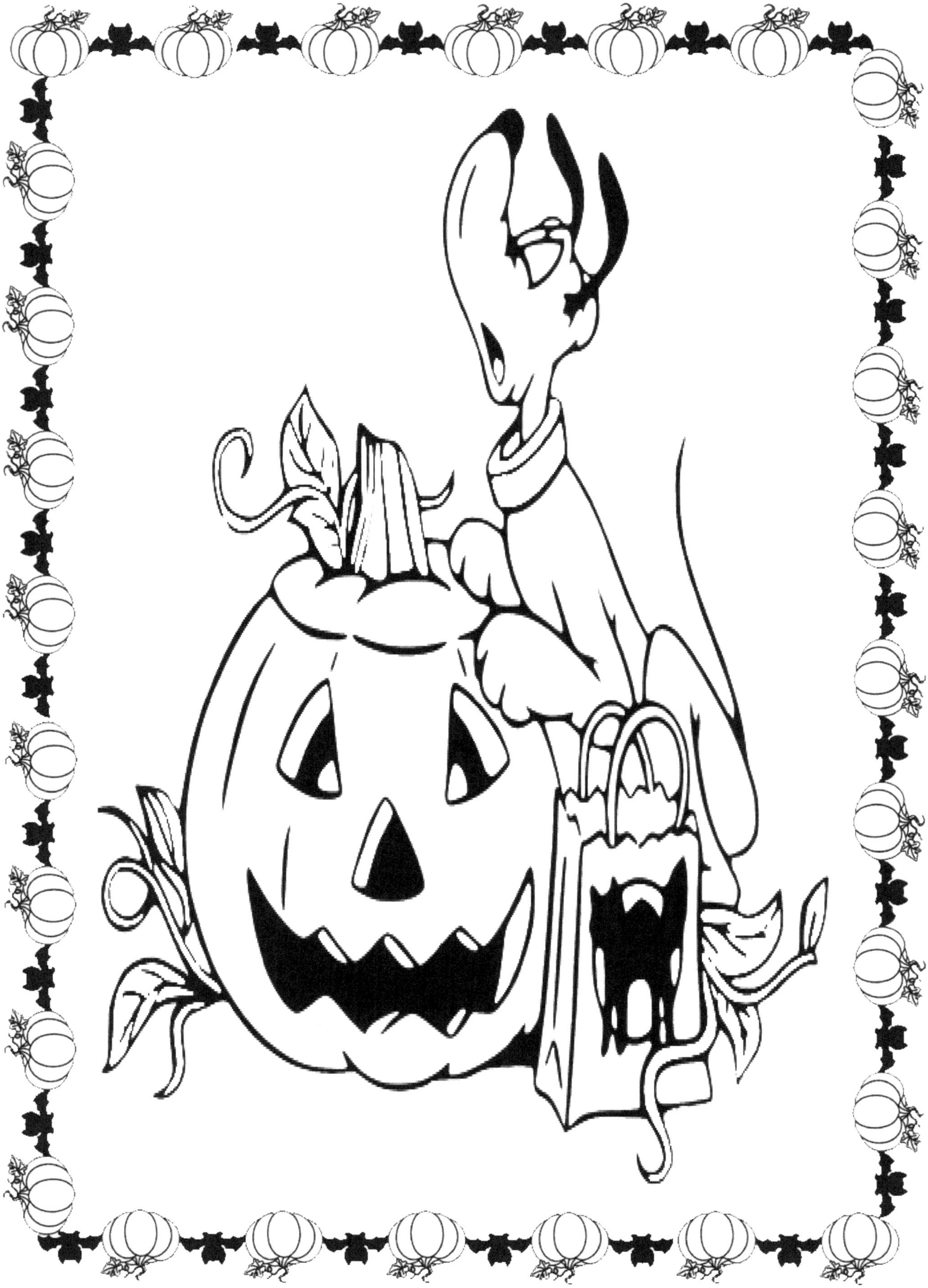

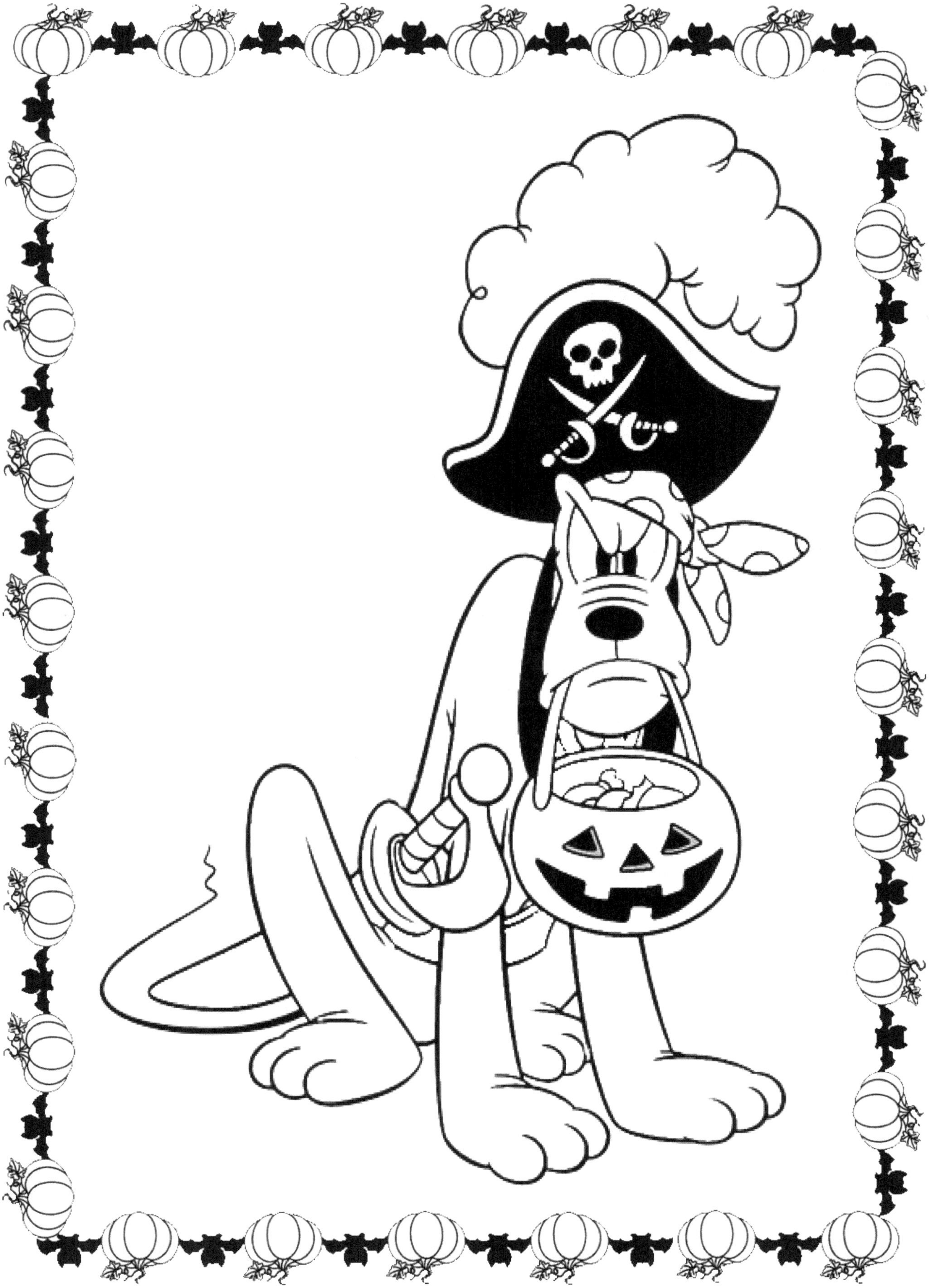

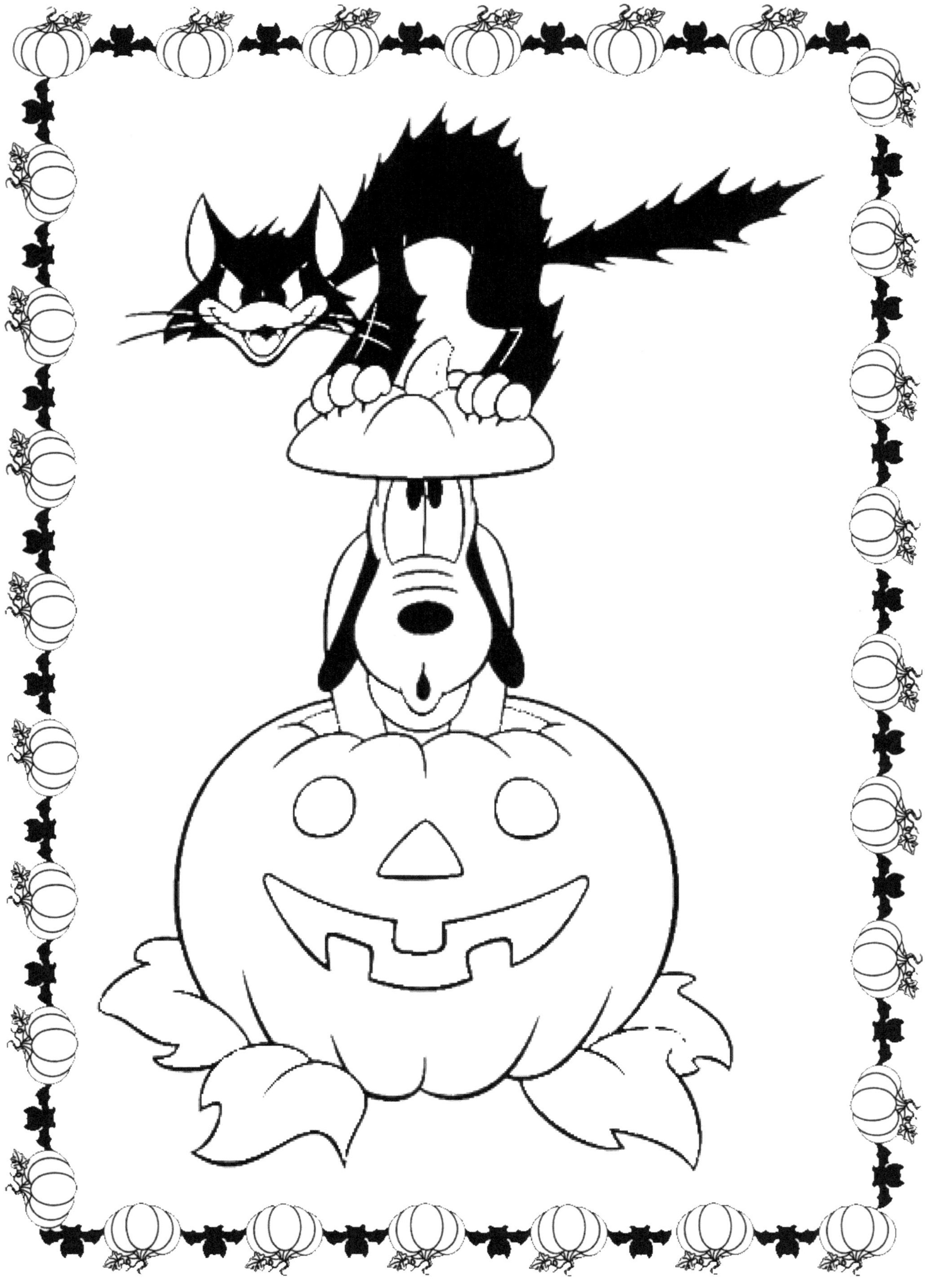

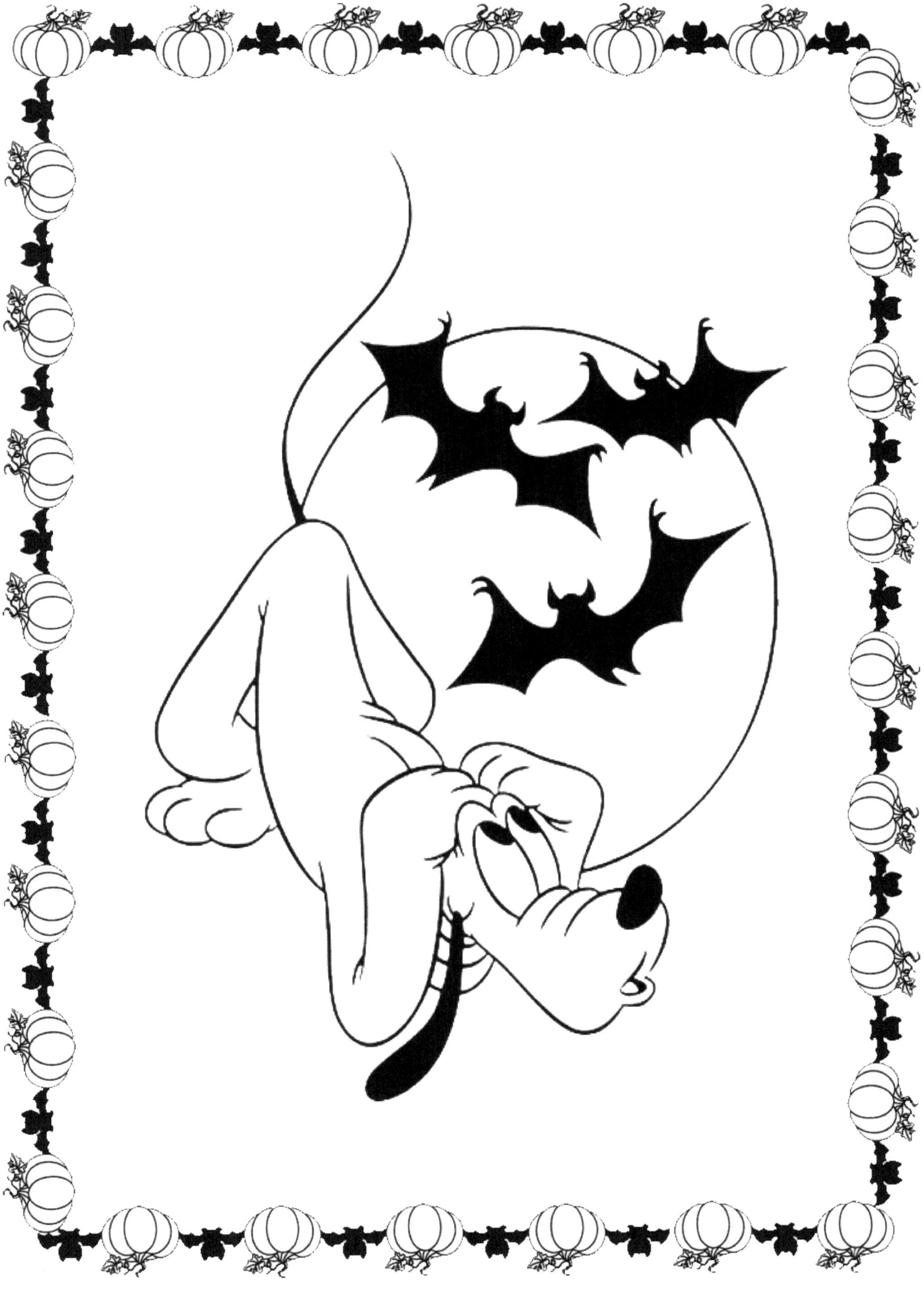

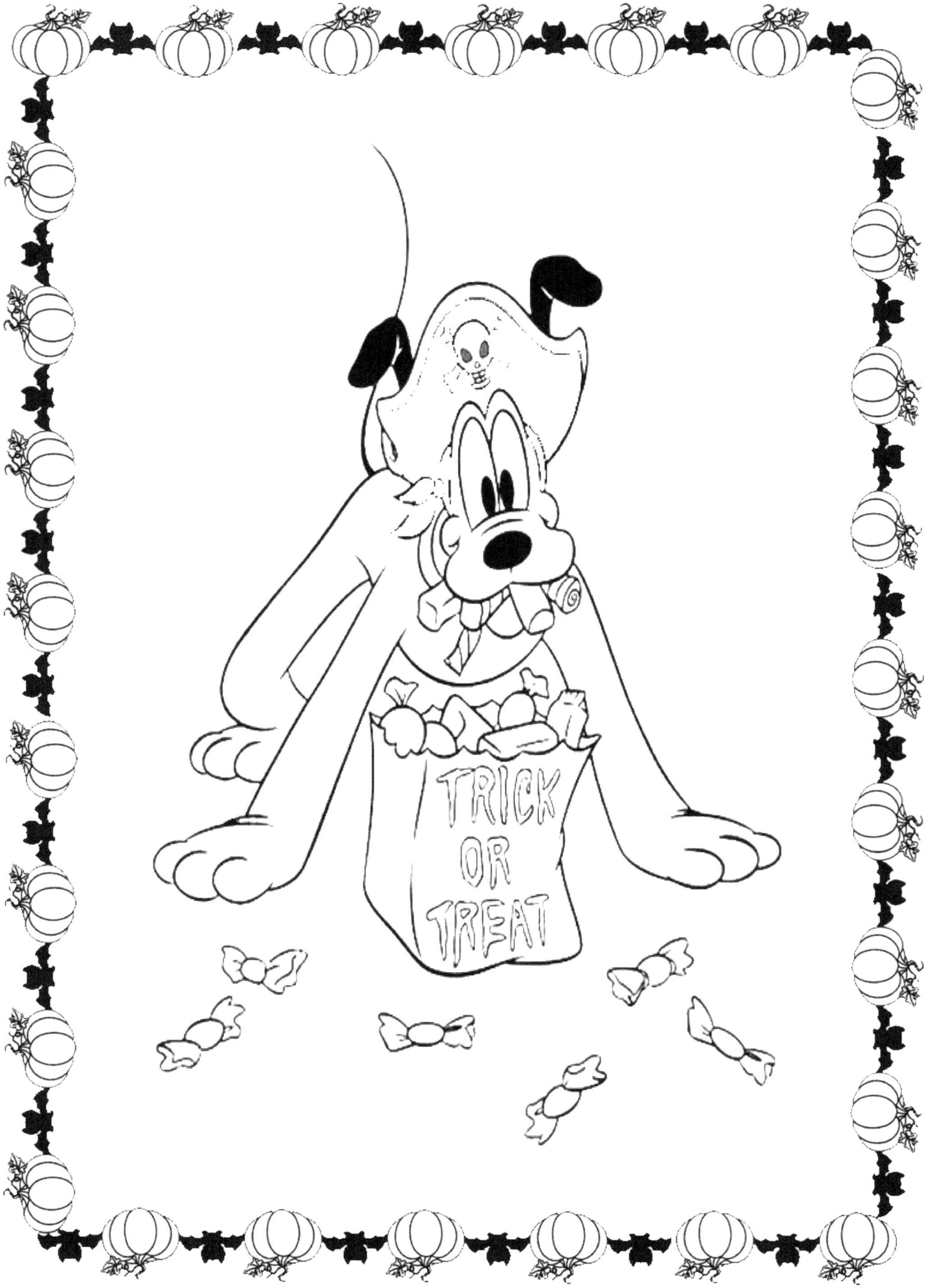
TRICK
OR
TREAT

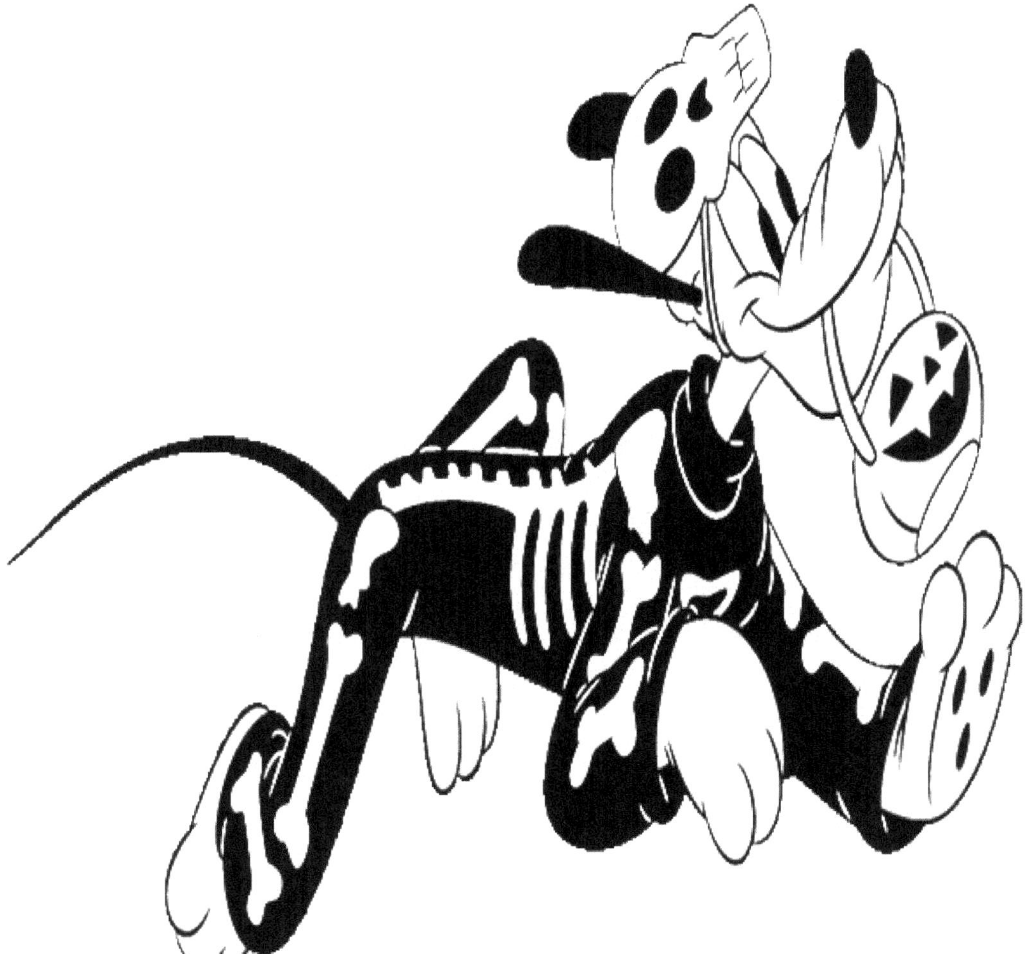

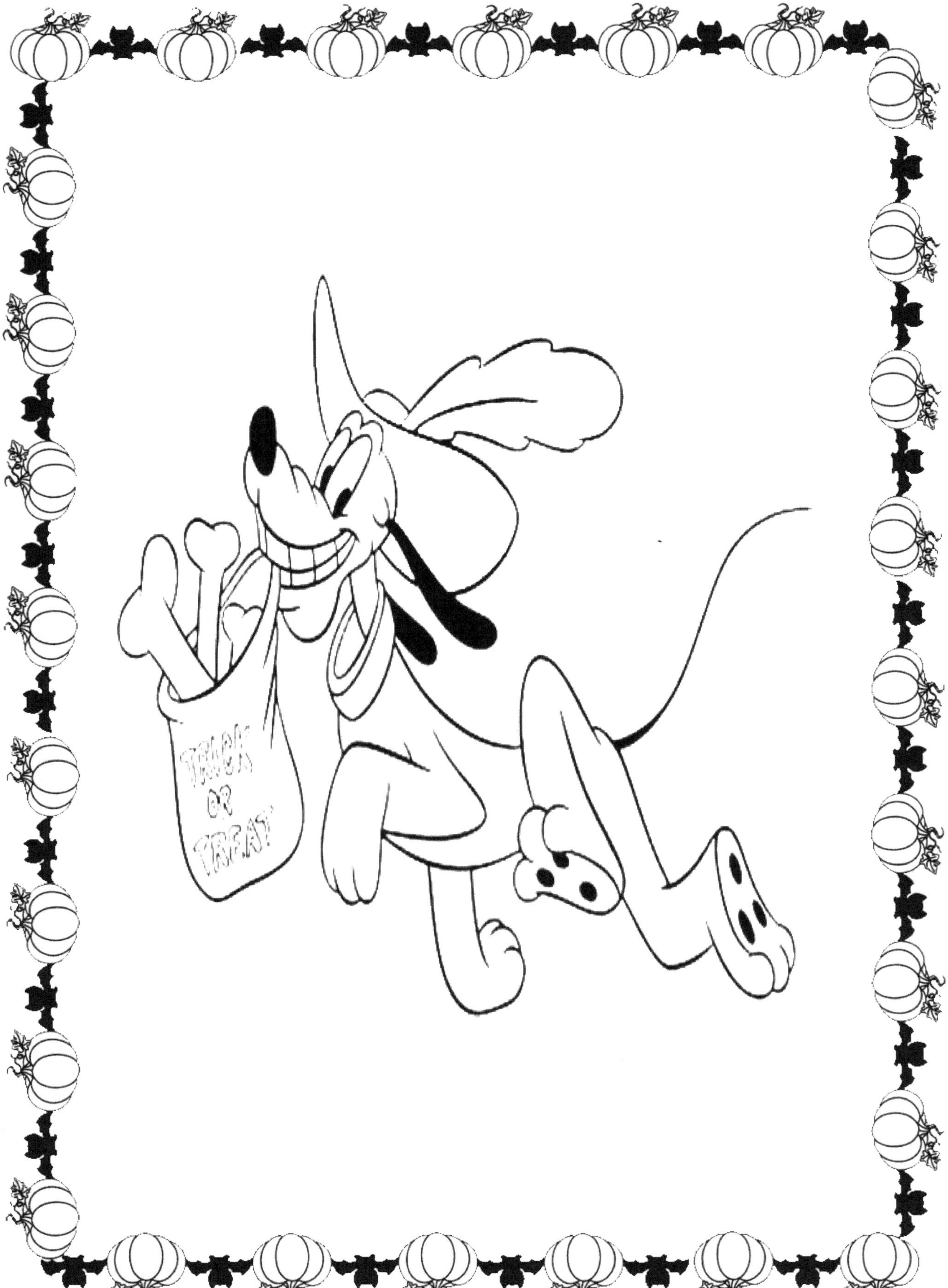
TRICK OR TREAT

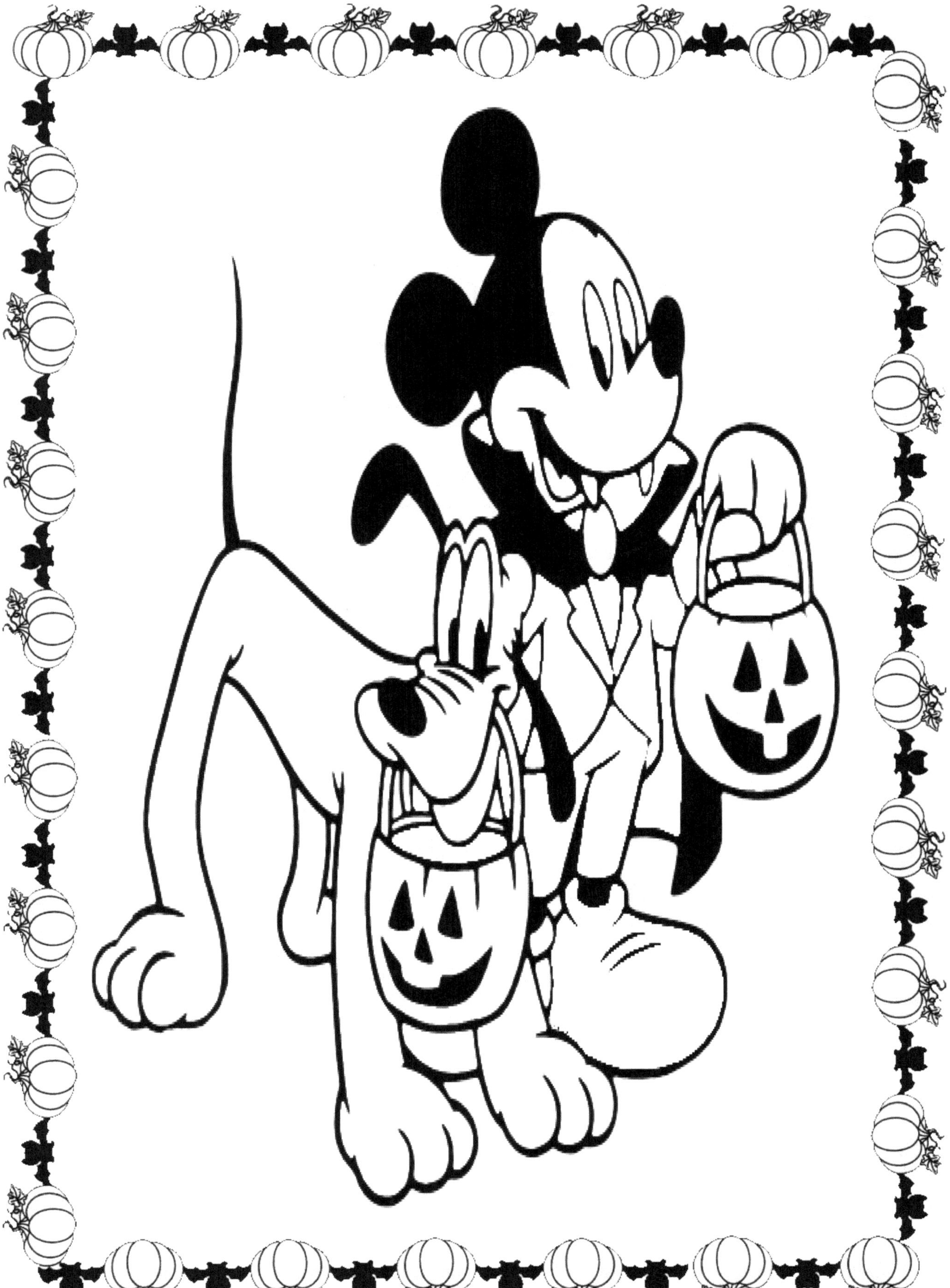

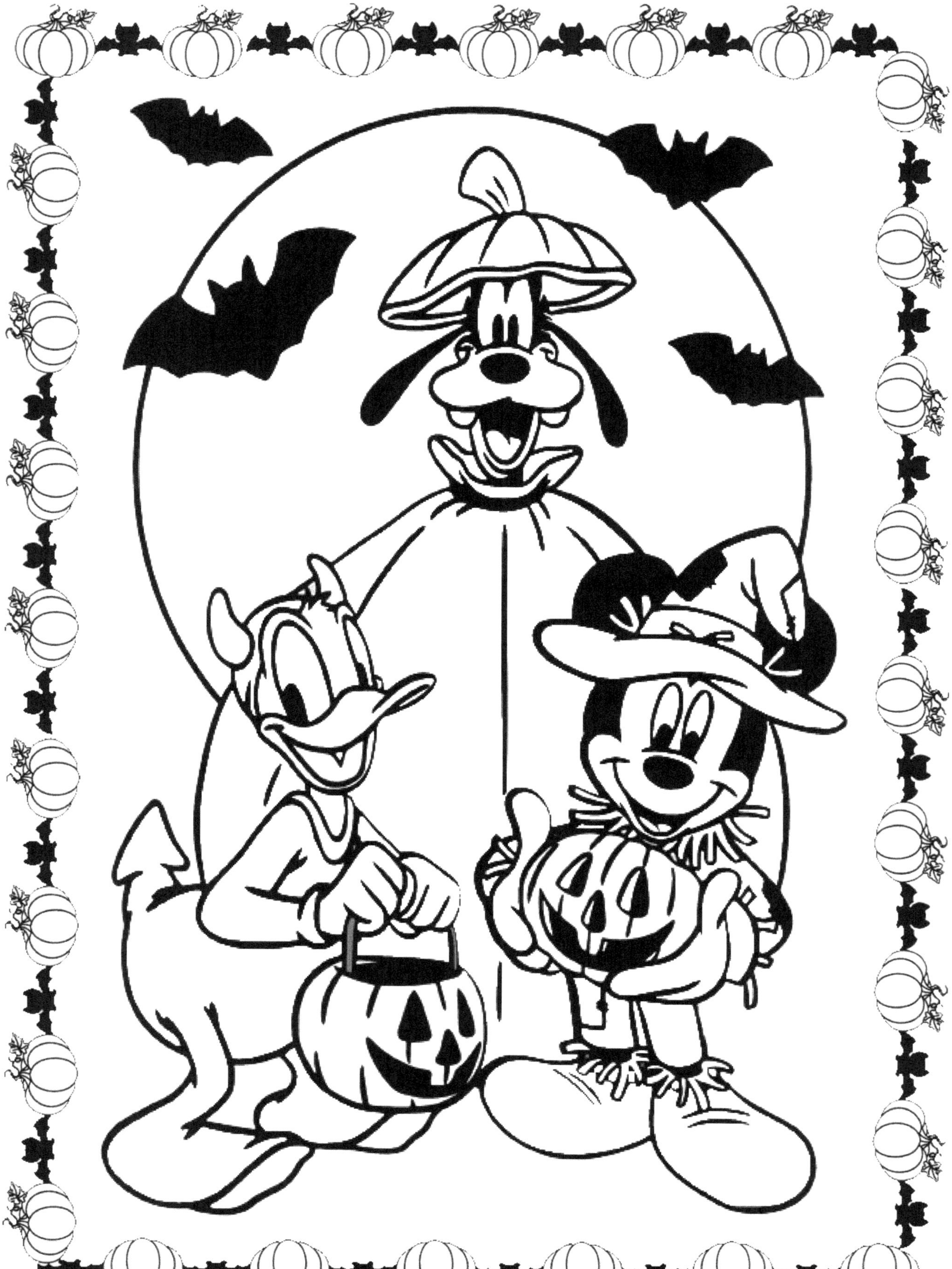

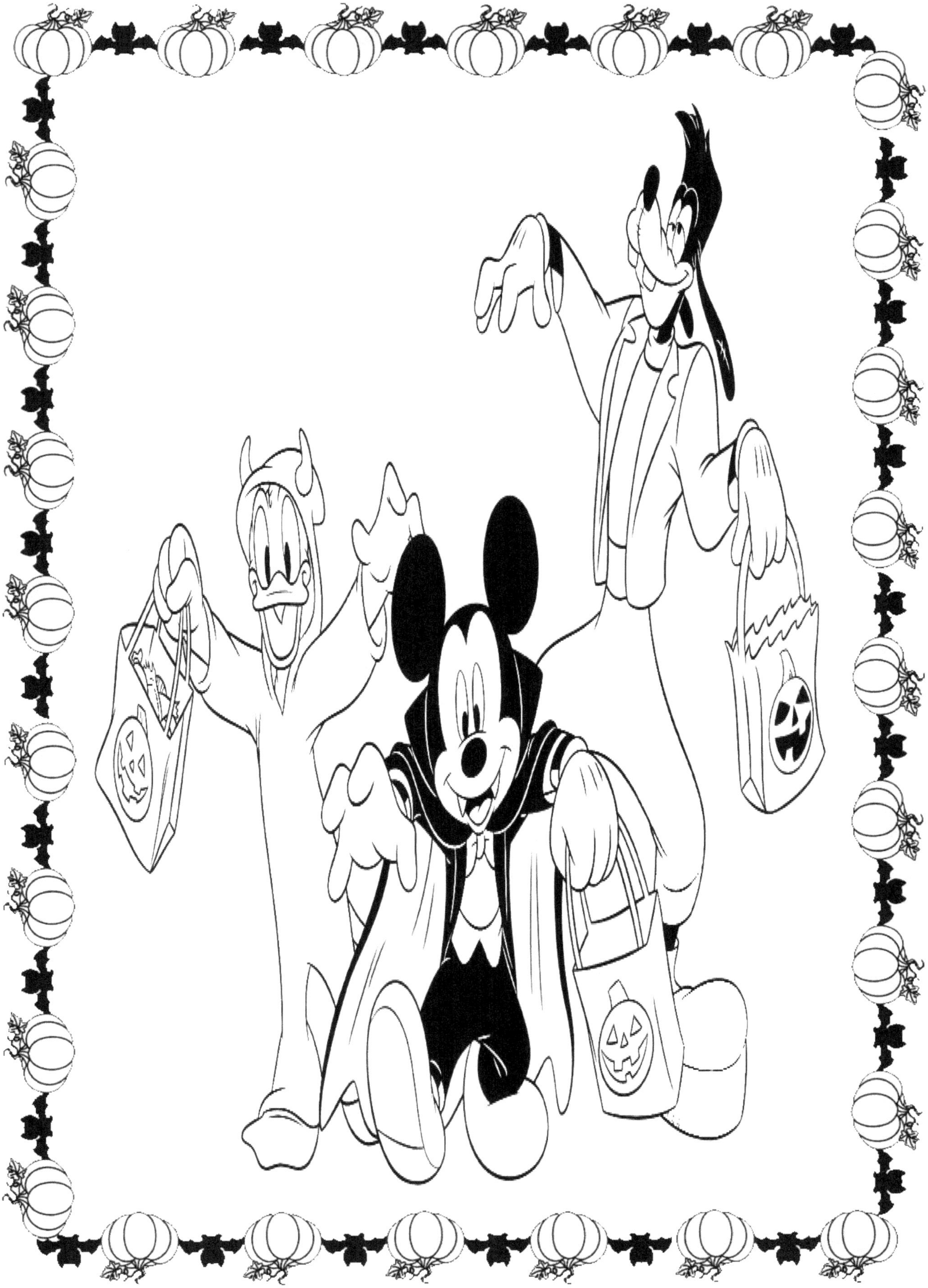

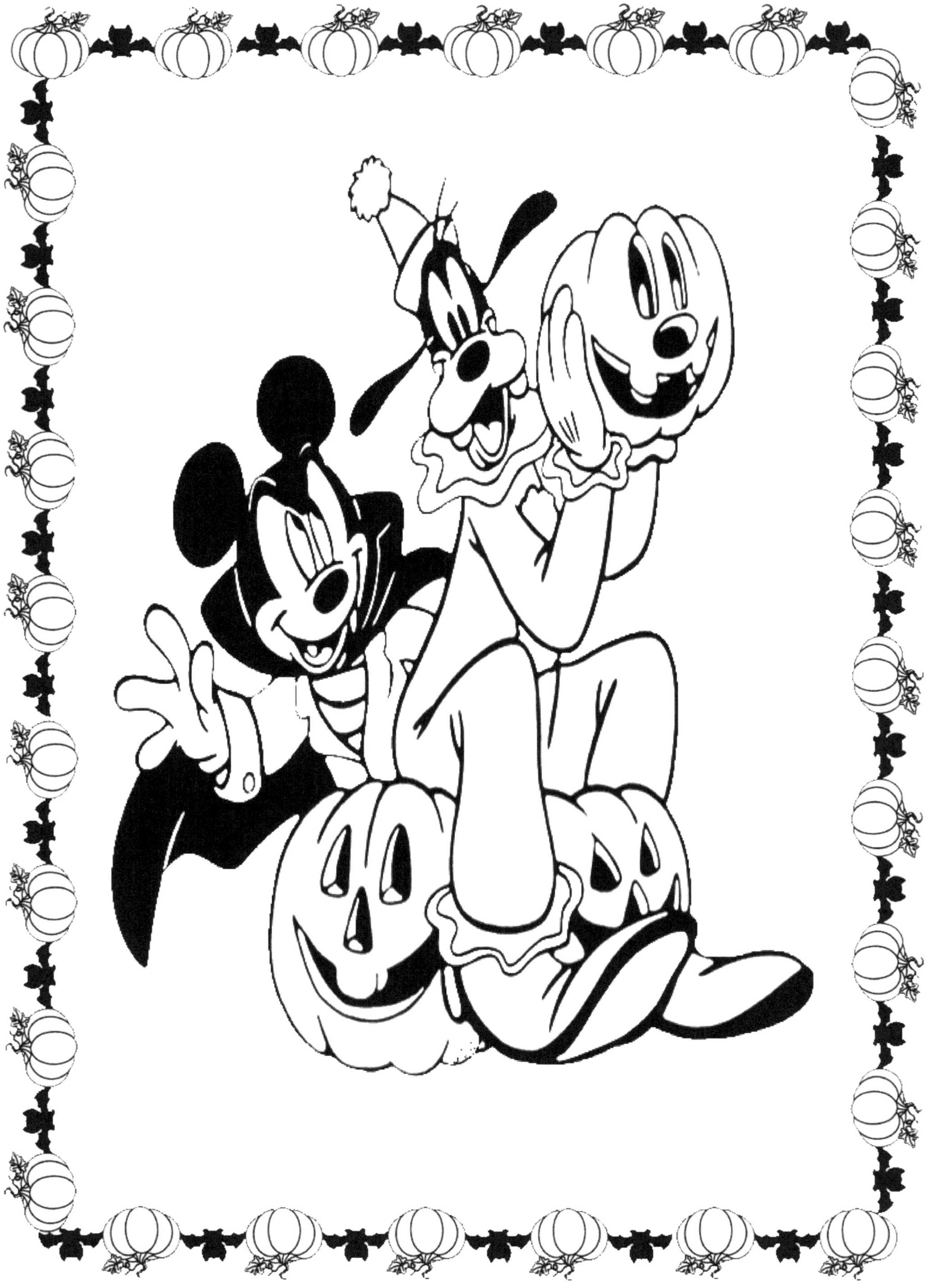

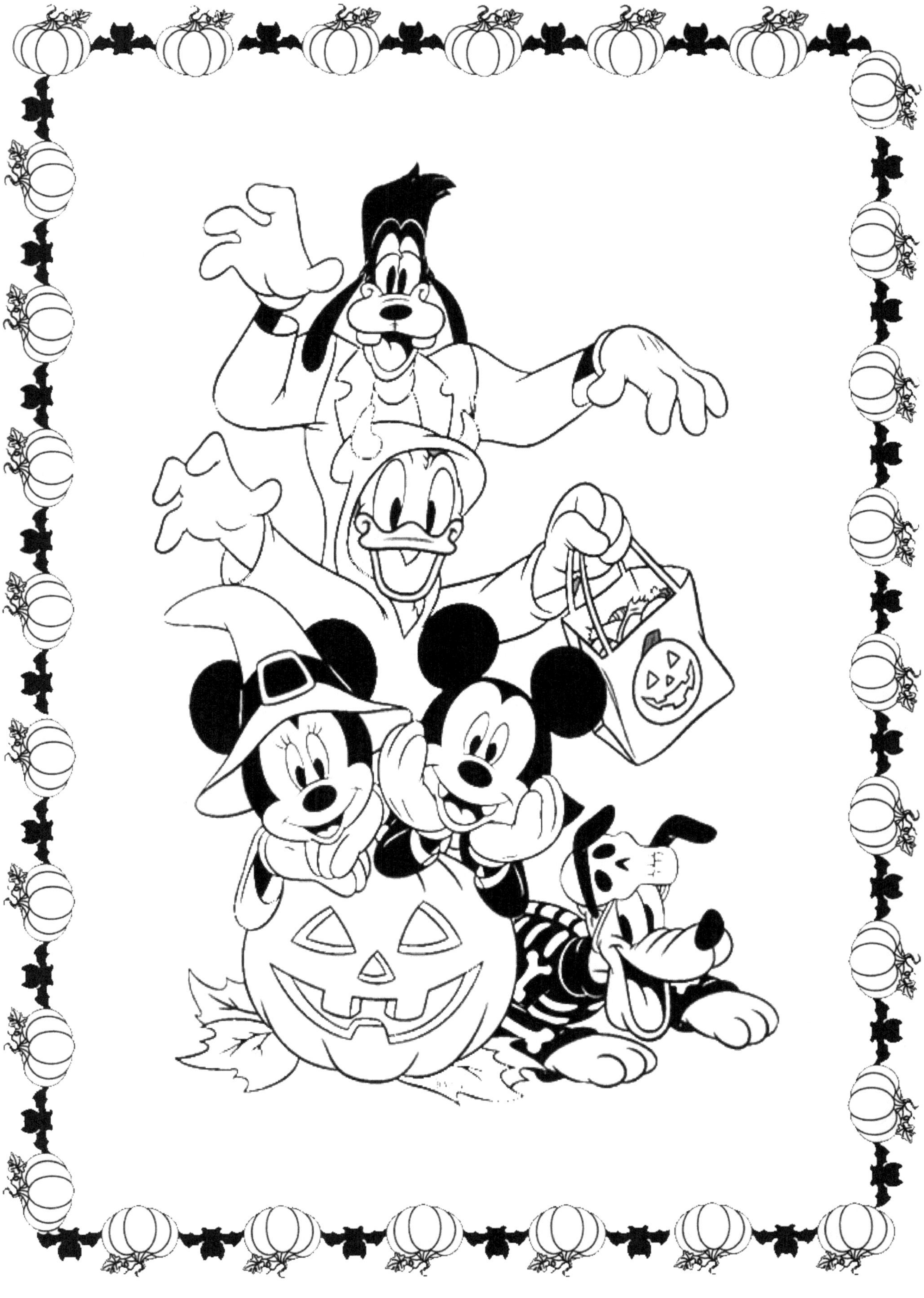

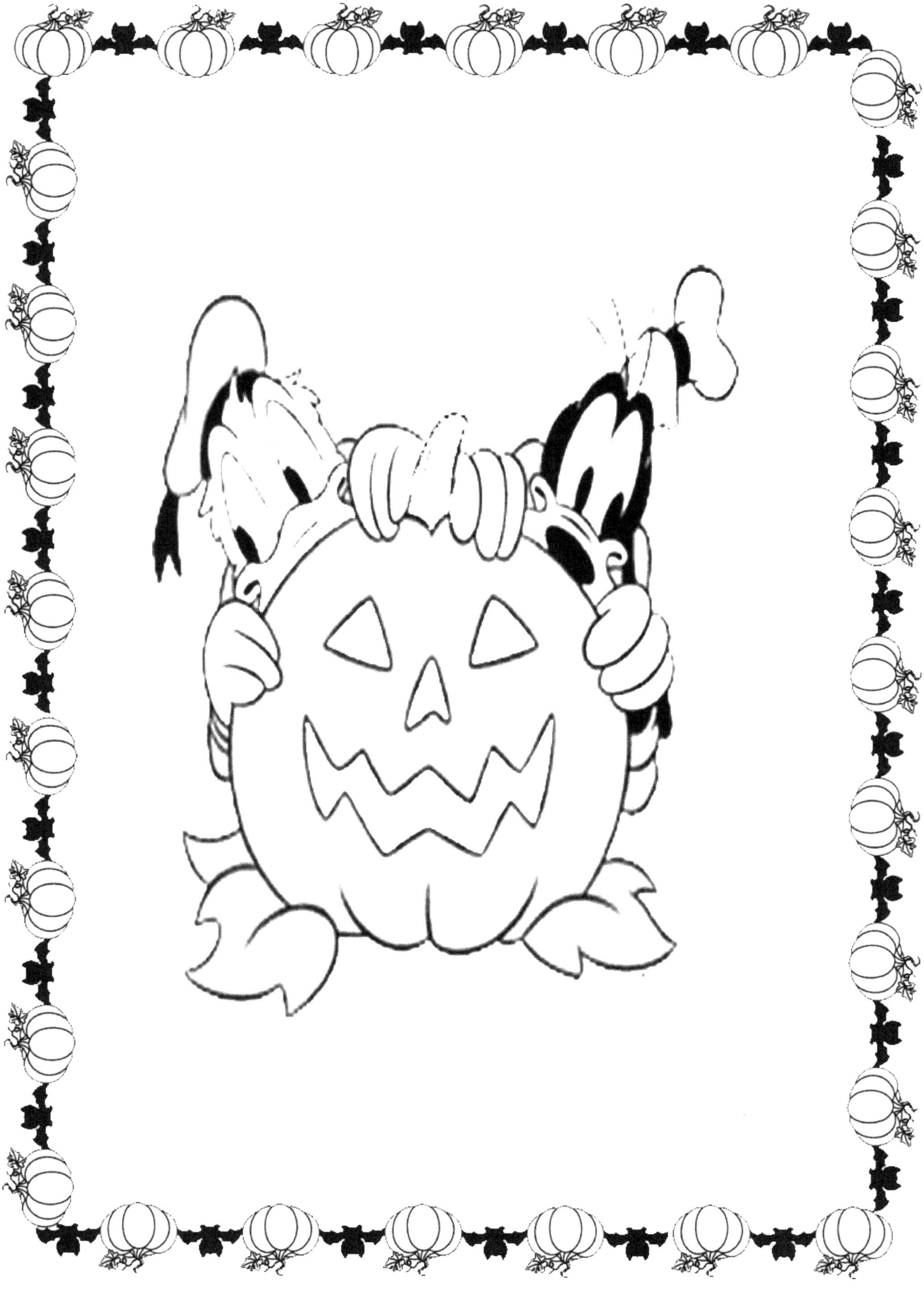

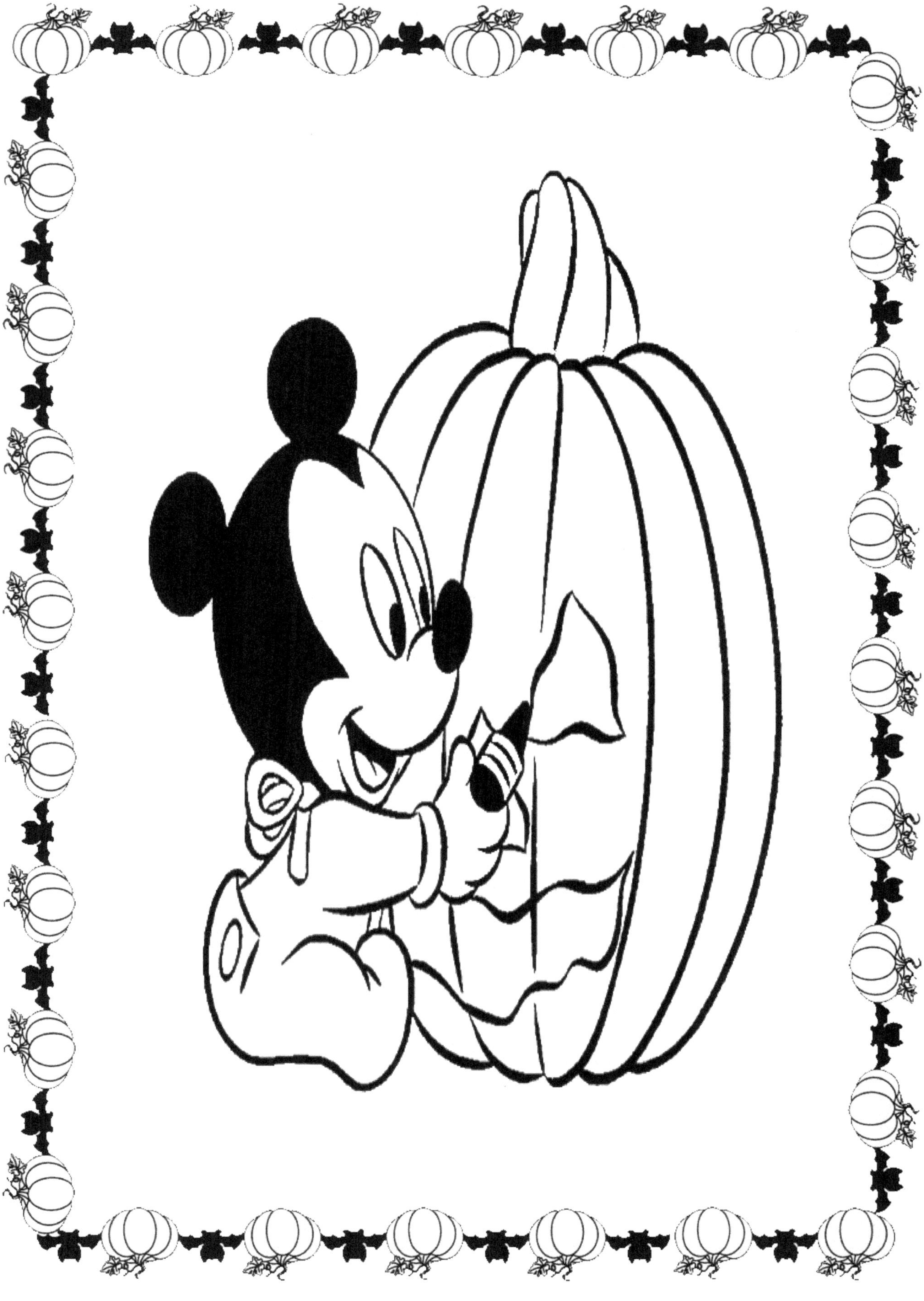

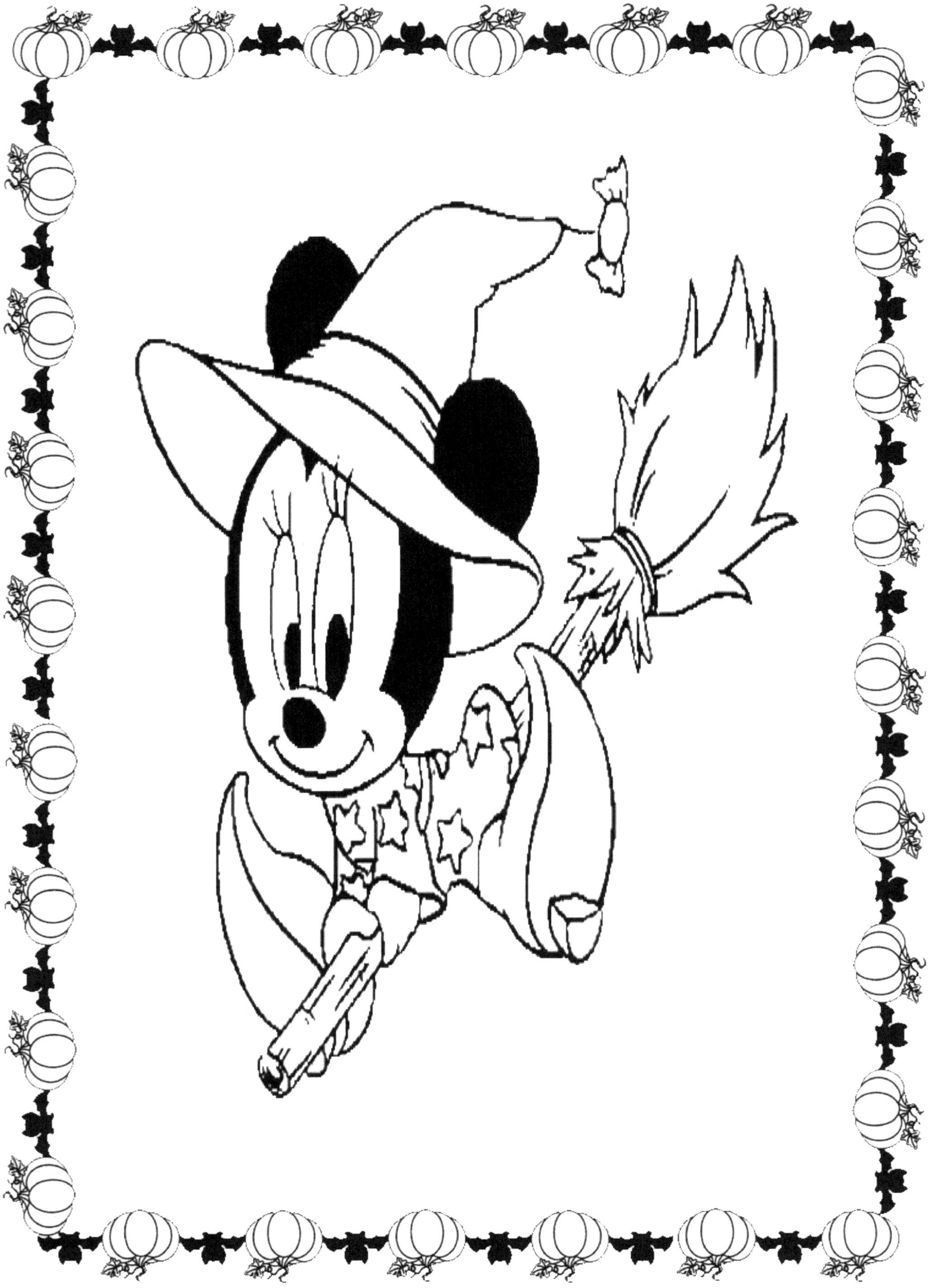

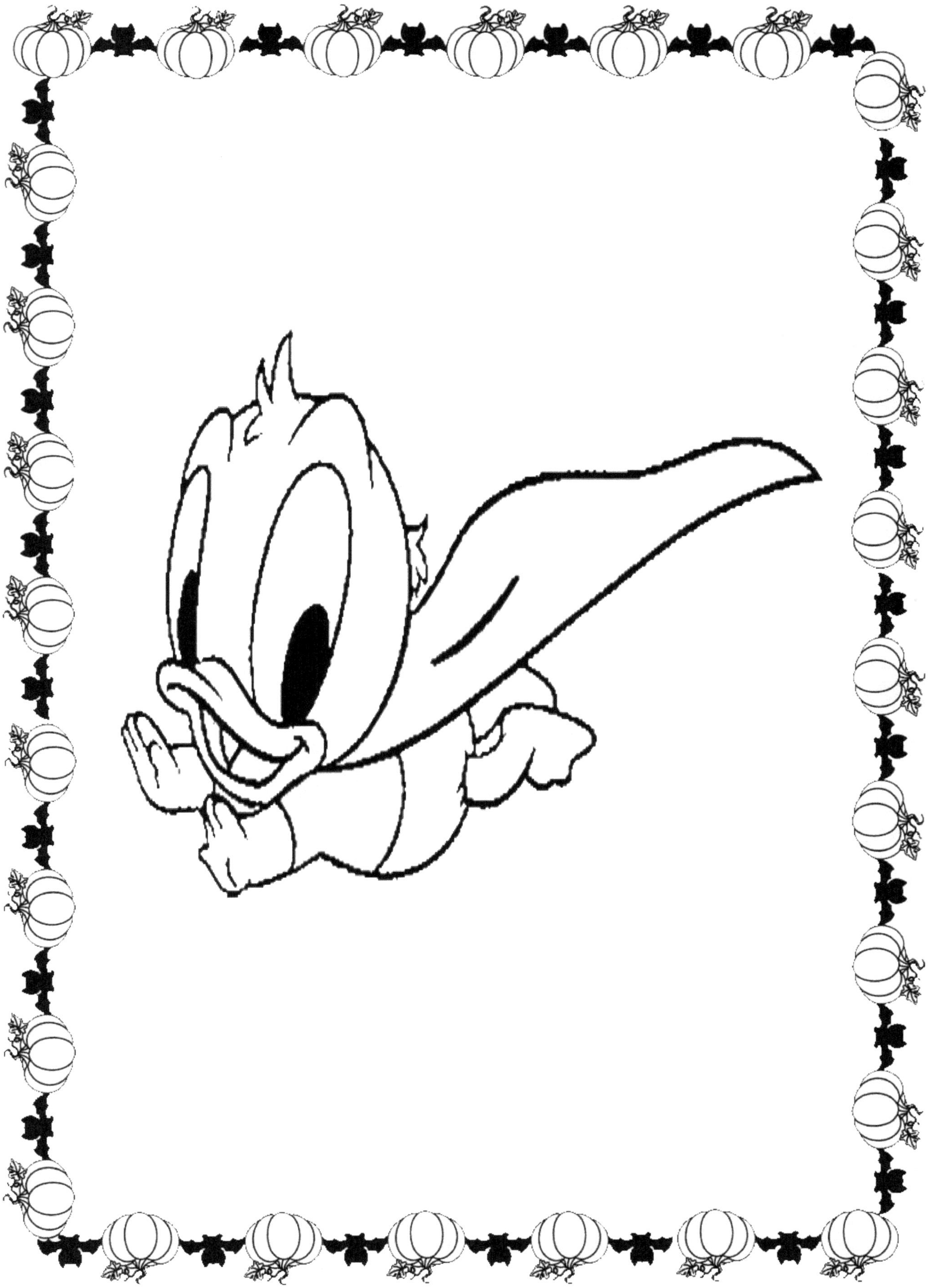

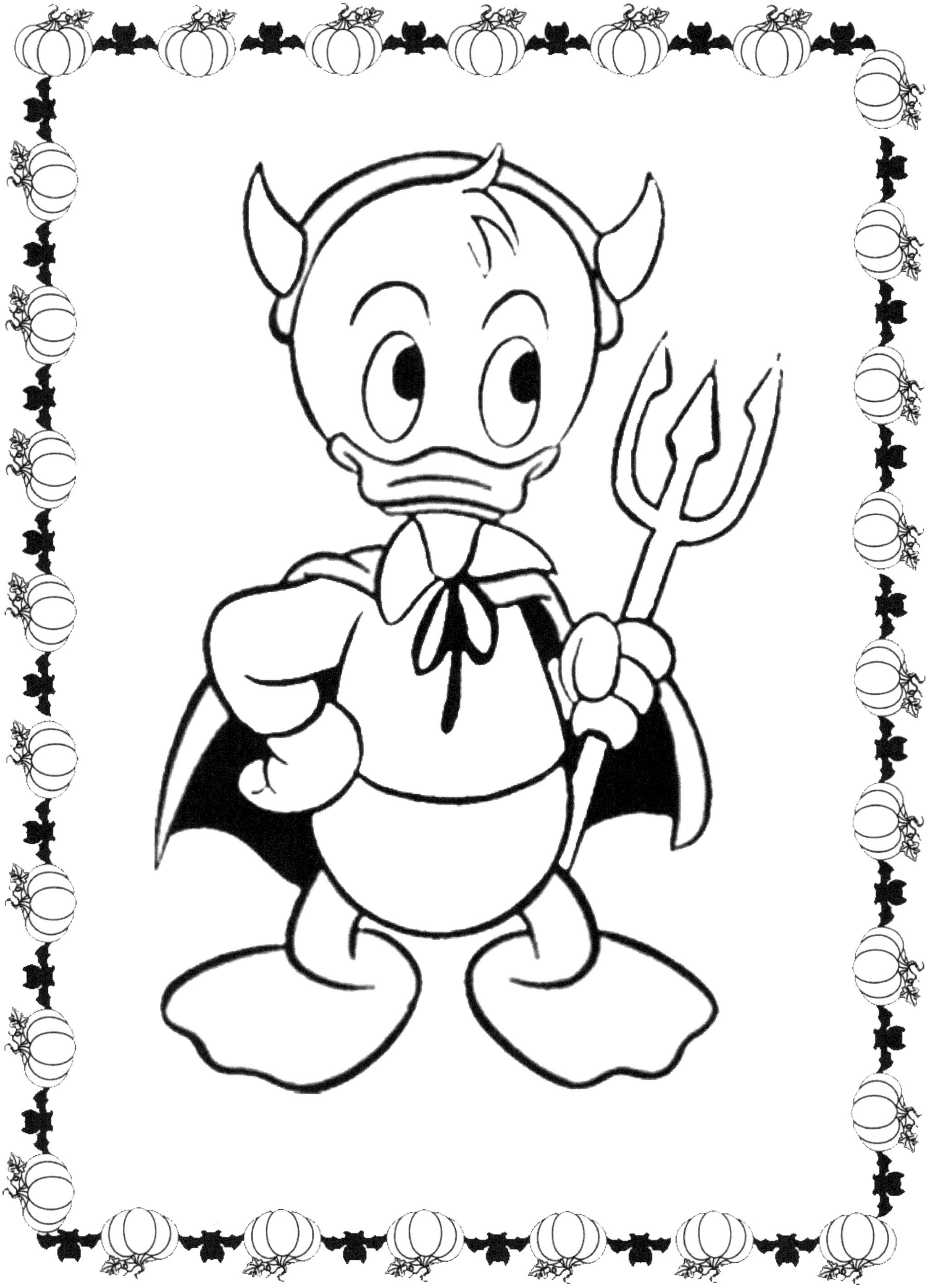

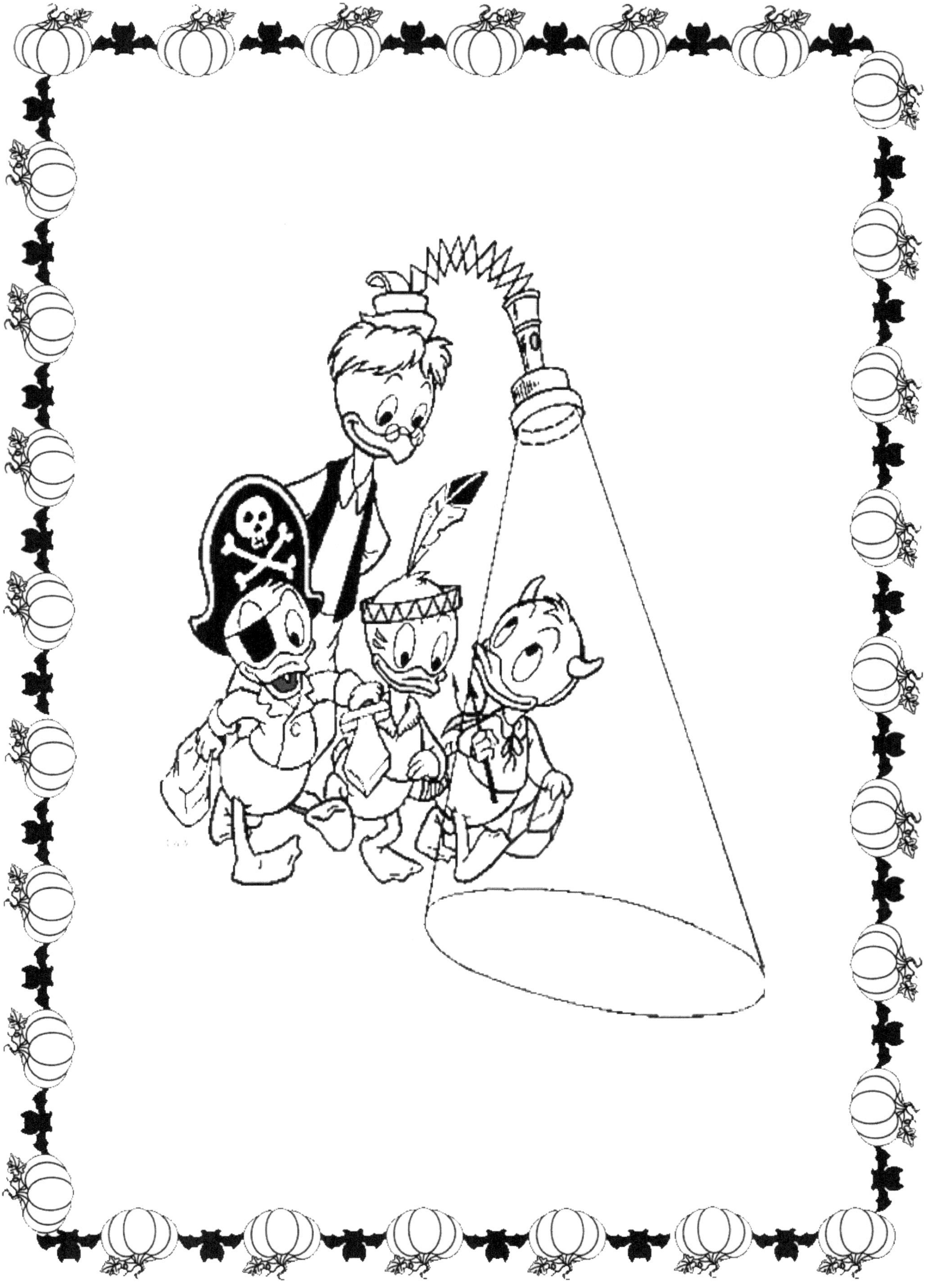

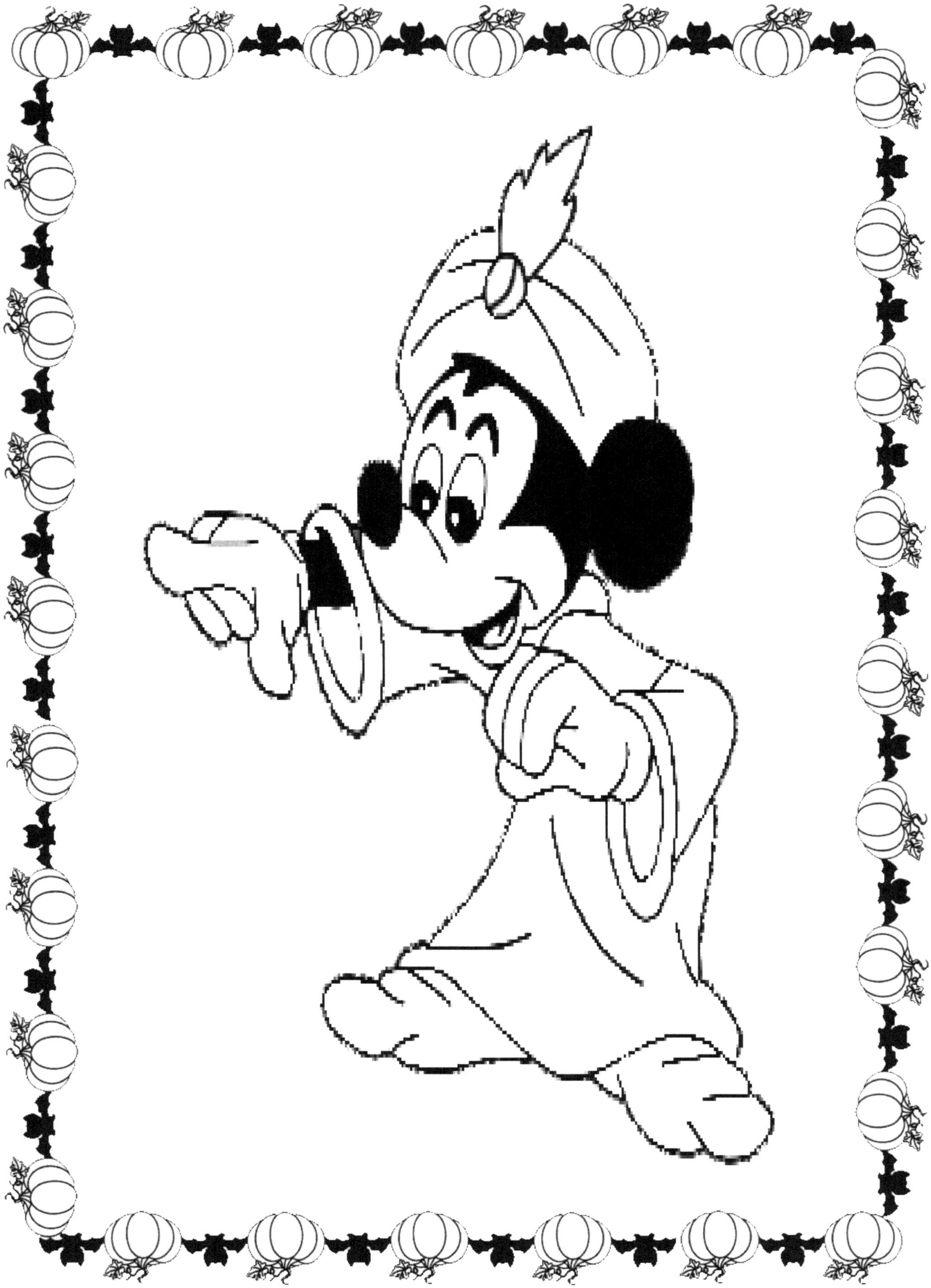

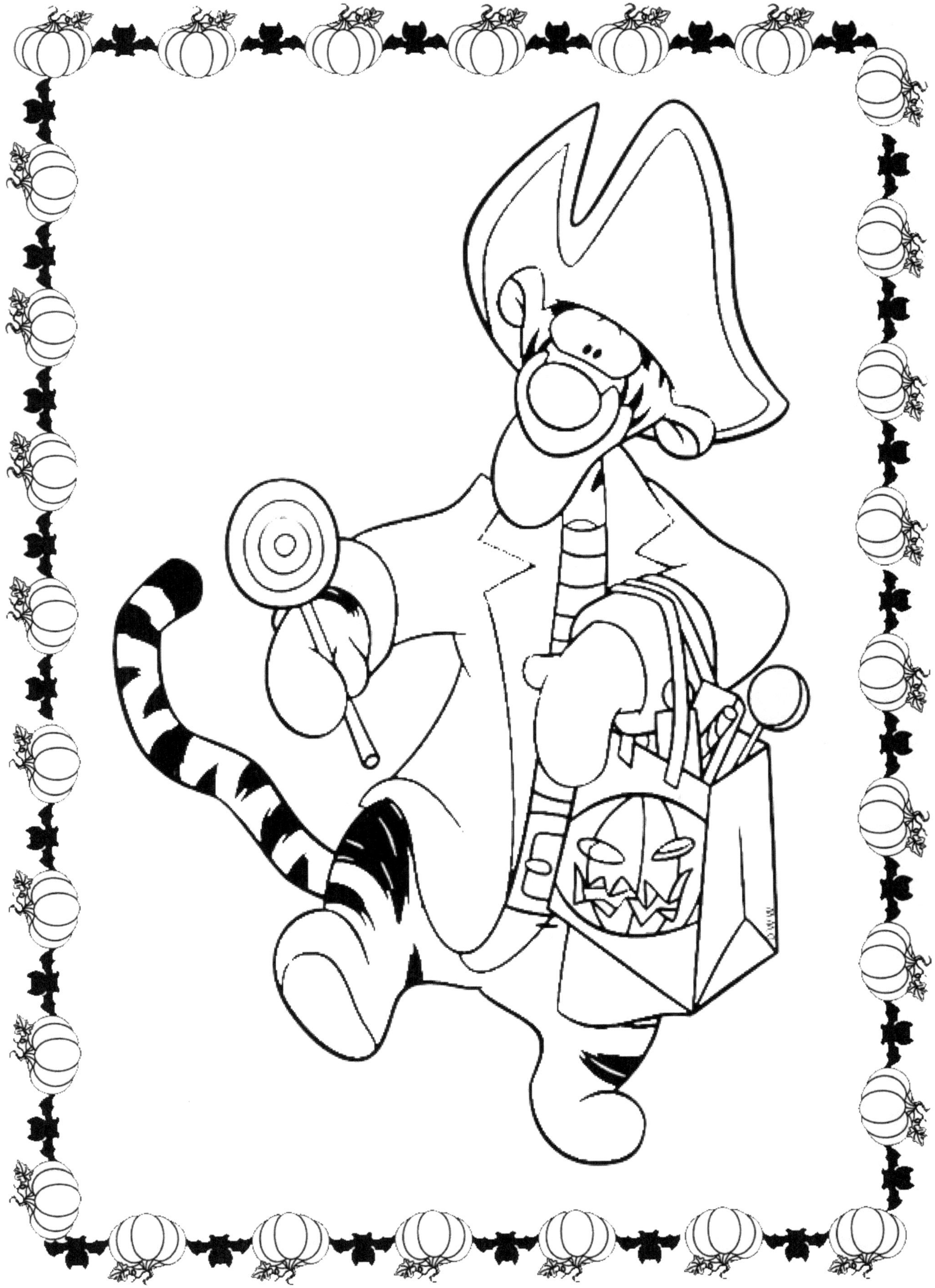

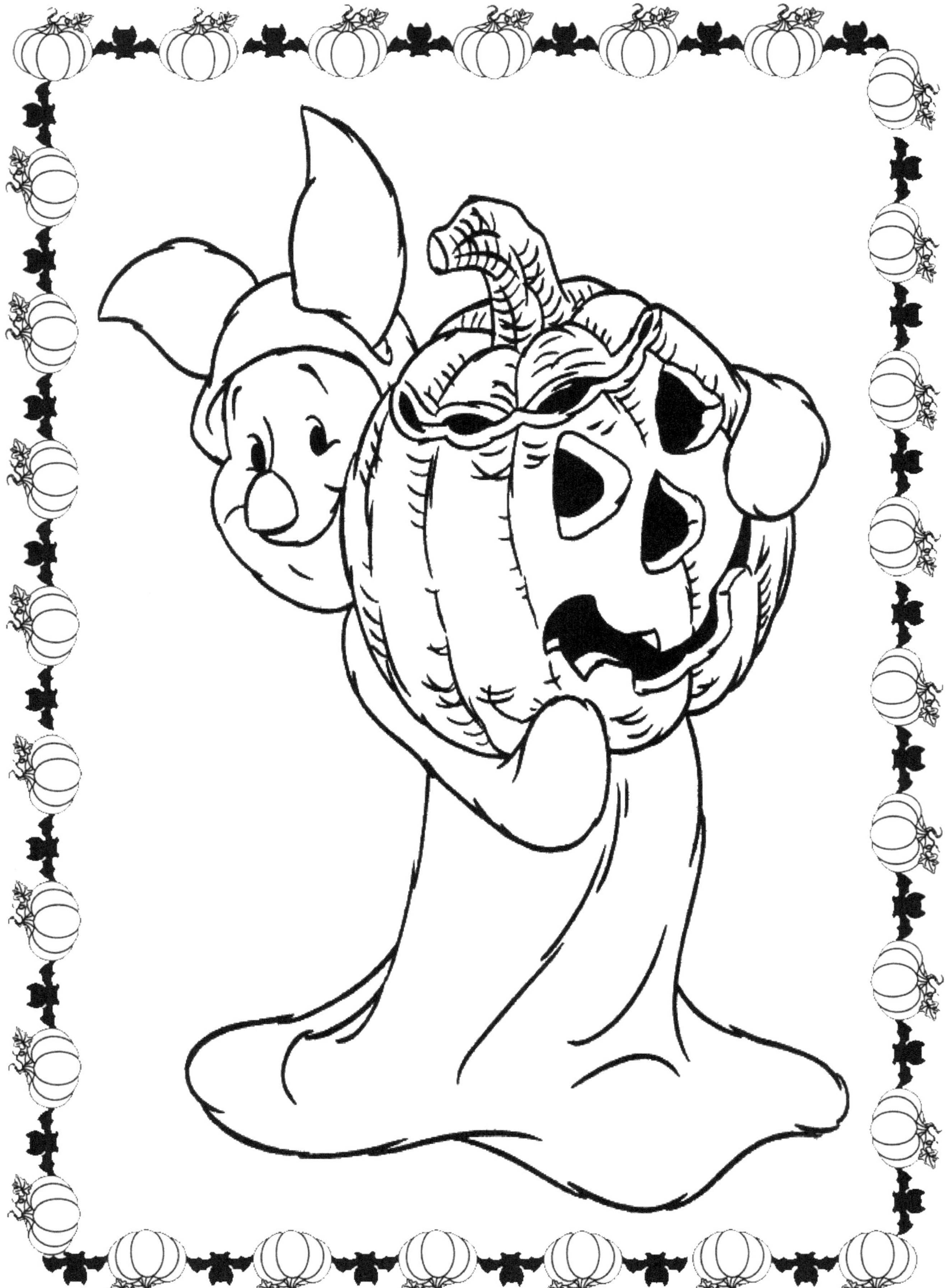

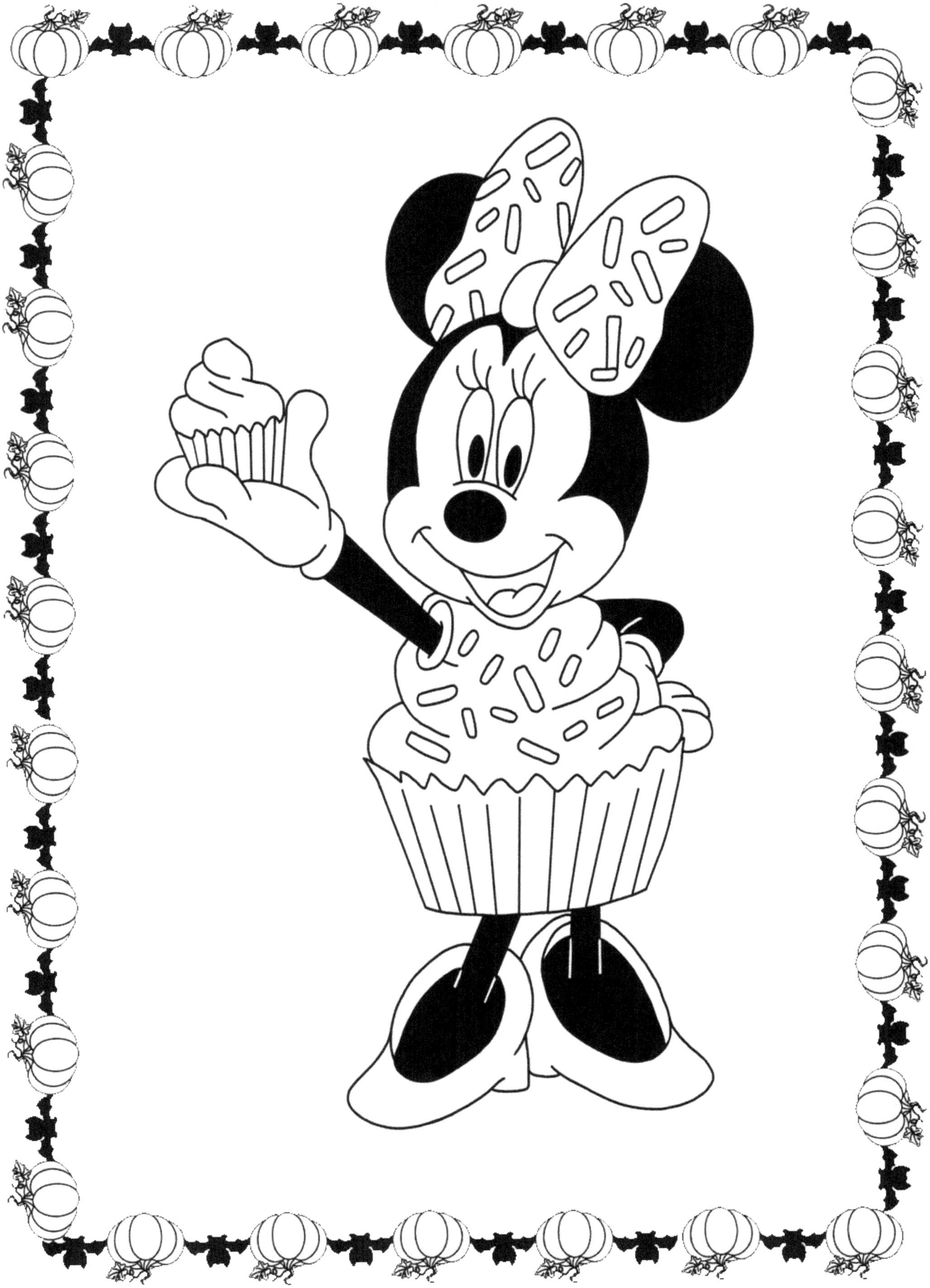

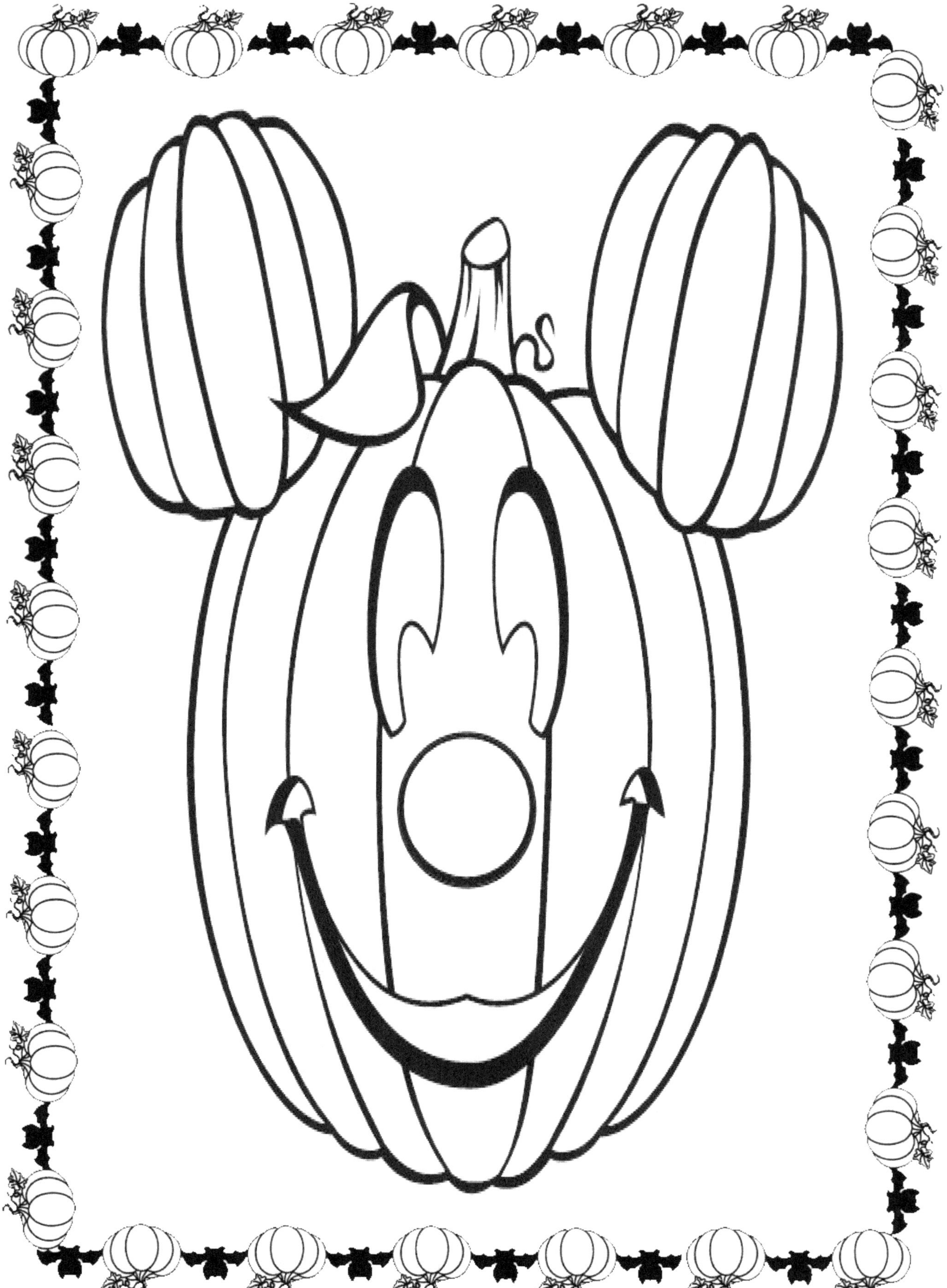

Printed in the USA
CPSIA information can be obtained
at www.ICGtesting.com
LVHW081549180924
791441LV00013B/532

9 798691 906015